Are you taking
OWNERSHIP
of your Career?

A guide for the Canadian
Independent Contractor

Nagy and Company Chartered Accountants
Suite 101, 5917 1A Street SW
Calgary, Alberta T2H 0G4
Phone: 403.209.2248 Fax: 403.539.2248
Website: www.ncca.co

Produced by:

FriesenPress

Suite 300 – 852 Fort Street
Victoria, BC, Canada V8W 1H8

www.friesenpress.com

Distributed to the trade by The Ingram Book Company

Are you taking
OWNERSHIP
of your Career?

A guide for the Canadian
Independent Contractor

Dennis R. Dowling, B.Com.,CPA,CA,CFP (CA – Alberta)

Table of Contents

To Linda, my loving wife of 43 years and counting who always seems to forgive my daily sins and cheesy jokes and provides me with inspiration to do my best in everything I undertake.

AND

To Tom Johnson, my late friend and colleague who found the stress and strain of the work we do too much to bear. Your advice remains in my heart.

Nota Bene (Pay Attention)

This book is designed as a guide for any Canadian contemplating or commencing work as an independent contractor. What is an independent contractor? From my standpoint, it basically refers to someone who is self-employed, providing a service and is essentially at the "Me Inc." stage. Although many of the issues and concerns relate to someone who is operating a business with several employees, or someone who is selling a product, the book is for the benefit of those selling their time that are operating as the sole shareholder/director or doing so with the assistance of their spouse. Having said this, there are people who may be operating as independent contractors in selling their time and they also sell a product. For example: a photographer may provide his services to do a photo shoot and be paid a fee for that service. In addition, the photographer may also sell the resulting prints, framing and albums that result from the photo shoot as part of his service.

Throughout the book, I will alternatively refer to the independent contractor as a consultant, a contractor or as a freelance contractor. All phrases are interchangeable. Many people often think of someone operating in one of the construction trades when they hear the phrase contractor. They think of the house builder, the plumber, or the electrician etc. I have found that a lot of contractors want to be referred to as "consultants" to distinguish themselves from a trade contractor. In fact, many trades people do operate as independent contractors, but they are only one facet of the group.

"Size matters not. Look at me. Judge me by my size, do you? Hmm? Hmm." – Yoda

Over the years, I've had a number of my clients indicate that they felt their small business was of little or no consequence. I caution you not to think this way. Don't think that just because your company doesn't have many employees and a large office that it is not important. Your company represents what you are doing with your career! That should have a major importance for you and your family.

Do not ever underestimate the importance of your company. Your business may not have a lot of employees or a lot of customers. That does not mean that there are not complications that require your constant attention. You do need to get proper financial advice, properly manage your record keeping and look to invest your funds prudently in order for you to succeed.

One of my former clients just declared bankruptcy. Throughout the period during which he was my client, he was one of my highest grossing clients. He annually withdrew through dividends, more than the average client would gross in fees each year. This client failed to properly manage his cash, spending it as he went rather than setting amounts aside to meet his liabilities, and funding his future cash requirements.

Why? (Did I Write This Book)

At the end of November 2011, I sold my accounting practice in order to retire. My practice represented the Edmonton, Alberta office of DNTW Chartered Accountants, LLP which is a national Chartered Accounting firm that I co-founded with Adrian Nagy from Calgary, Alberta.

My late father had often told me that you can't retire to do nothing. I didn't have any specific plans except to get away from the daily stress which meant to stop working at what I had been doing for the past forty years. Despite having been supported my entire life by the accounting profession, I had pretty much reached the end of my desire to do that work. No question, I was looking to tap into my artistic side as it seemed that there had never been enough time to do that. I thought I would like to finally learn how to play the guitar. I have three guitars and I had taken lessons periodically over the years. It seemed that I would just be starting to sound decent, at least to me, and then work would pull me away. I also thought that I would like to relearn to play the piano, so I bought a new electronic piano and I started playing it faithfully for about four months. Work again pulled me away when I had to invoice the remainder of my work in progress. I had been delayed in doing this because a software problem came up and it took me three months to get the time and billing program functional again.

I have always had a desire to do some writing. I have had it in my mind that I would like to write fictional mystery novels. As part of the day to day work, there are always tax letters and letters of recommendation to be written to and on behalf of my clients. I had also produced newsletters for my firm for several years, researching and writing the articles myself. Even recently, most of the frequently asked questions brochures that our firm provided for our independent contractor clients were researched and written by me. In fact, several of those brochures were used in forming the basis of this book.

Following my retirement, I considered starting a mystery novel, however I felt it would be more productive to write about something that I knew extremely well. At one point I had grown somewhat disillusioned with my accounting practice. It was at this point that I discovered working with independent contractors as a target market. This finding rejuvenated me as I found it was so rewarding to work with these consultants, and I could help them to such a great degree. My experience comprises approximately 15 years of working with independent contractors, delivering numerous seminars for independent contractors, and having spent approximately 14,000 hours in face-to-face meetings across my boardroom table with independent contractors. This does not even consider the related phone calls and e-mails during that time. With this extensive experience, it seemed it would be more productive for me to start writing a book that would continue to benefit from the knowledge and experience that I could provide to people contemplating a change in their career. As it turns out, this was probably a good idea because I have found that writing a book requires a great deal more creativity than that required for a technical document.

From my standpoint, a secondary reason to write about independent contracting is that Canada Revenue Agency (at least one Quebec office of CRA) and Revenu Quebec have been waging a campaign against people operating as independent contractors. They have been assessing these contractors as "personal service businesses" which is explained in greater detail later in this book. Unfortunately, many contractors will read about the attack on them by the government and will abandon this relatively new way of working. I hope to dispel some of your fears through this book by explaining how you should set up your business. There are a few criteria that must be followed to insulate you from an inappropriate reassessment as a personal service business. It is not sufficient to set yourself up correctly; you must also walk the walk of being a contractor.

You need to approach life with a certain positive attitude. At some point you'll want to look back and ask yourself three questions and hopefully you will be able to answer yes to each. You'll want to ask yourself did I live, did I love and did I make a difference? It is the third question that I want to address in writing this book. I can look back at this point, and I know that I have made a significant difference in the lives and careers of many of my clients.

My advice over the years has helped numerous clients achieve a major financial nest egg that will lead them towards their goal of financial independence. It is in the writing of this book that I hope to pass along the same encouragement to many others, to "take ownership of your career."

Why? (Should You Read This Book)

What are the benefits to you in reading this book? In the book, both the financial advantages and the nonfinancial advantages of independent contracting have been demonstrated for the individual wanting to work as an independent contractor as well as the person who wants to make use of these skills being provided in this form of organization. I have discussed the skills beyond the technical ones which you will need to develop to be successful as an independent contractor. A comparison of the forms in which you can operate as an independent contractor has been made and the various expenses that you can claim have been detailed. Not wanting to over empha-size the positive, I have also addressed a number of the risks or con-cerns that an independent contractor may face. Independent con-tractors become high earners, but a high income does not lead you to wealth and financial independence. Therefore, I have included several chapters on how you should manage your financial assets.

The contents of the book as listed above represent features of this book. The benefits, however, are what will make a difference for you in reading the book. The Tax Act and Canada Revenue Agency have a very narrow view of whether an individual is an employee or an independent contractor. In reading this book, you'll develop an understanding that although there are significant financial advantages of operating as an independent contractor, there are also many reasons why both an individual and a person paying for his services would prefer that the relationship between them is that of a contract for service rather than a contract of service. Understanding these advantages and preparing a proper independent consulting contract, as outlined in the book, will provide you with the knowledge and confidence that you need to operate successfully.

This book provides you with the knowledge to properly set up your business to realize the maximum tax and financial opportunities available. This includes how to structure your company as well as knowing what expenses are available for you to claim as business expenses. You will learn what things you need to be on the lookout for to ensure that you do not get tripped up along the way.

Relative to operating as an employee, the individual operating as an independent contractor will accumulate much more cash and this will happen fairly quickly. This book sets out the importance of properly managing the excess funds to ensure that you have the money to pay taxes and other liabilities as they arise, as well as how to pay yourself in a tax efficient manner.

It is these benefits that will ensure your success as an independent contractor and enable you to take ownership of your career.

Acknowledgements

You might notice that I have not included a bibliography for this book. It is not really an oversight; it is just that I have had so many various sources in learning about the financial needs of an independent contractor. With two office moves since starting work with independent contractors and about four changes in computer systems, I have lost much of my original reference materials. What I have addressed with this book is more a compilation of my experiences and interactions with my clients over the past 15 years, as well as referrals to documents which I wrote myself during that time frame. Credit for 95% of the book goes to the many clients who listened and benefitted from the advice I gave them as well as those who didn't listen. Those who didn't listen just made for more stories that would help the rest.

This does not mean that there are not specific individuals that I need to acknowledge and thank for their assistance.

First and foremost, I need to acknowledge and thank Mr. George Wall of "CA4IT." George is a Chartered Accountant and the owner of CA4IT which stands for, "Chartered Accountants for Information Technologists." In 1996, George was operating an accounting practice in Toronto, Ontario, that was working exclusively with independent contractors in the information technology field. He had developed a unique approach to the marketing and servicing of independent contractors and was looking to create an association of accounting firms across Canada that were prepared to specialize in this market, using his techniques. I met with Mr. Wall in the summer of 1996 and became the first associate office in June of 1997. It was this association that prompted me to change focus of my accounting practice and become successful in working with independent contractors.

Out of the CA4IT Association, I developed many friendships and received a great deal of encouragement. Primary among my Associates were Tom Johnson who operated the original Ottawa office and Adrian Nagy, who operated the Calgary office. During the initial meeting of the associate offices, Tom, Adrian and I spent some time together during which we hatched the idea of forming a national partnership.

Tom Johnson was a brilliant chartered accountant who built a significant practice of independent contractor clients while employed full time. Tom very shortly left his employment to operate his practice full-time. It was his unselfish devotion to his practice and his clients that led to a tragic end for him. Before this happened, we had commenced the first steps towards forming a partnership that consisted of the three offices. In the meantime, Tom and I contributed to the CA4IT Association by creating the frequently asked questions section of their website. The research that we put into this section of the website gave us both an in-depth knowledge of the requirements of independent contractors.

Without the assistance, hard work and persistence of Mr. Adrian Nagy, DNTW Chartered Accountants, LLP would never have come to fruition. With the passing of Tom Johnson, Adrian and I continued to pursue the establishment of a partnership of firms specializing in independent contractors. We formed the Alberta Chartered Accounting firm operating as "Chartered Accountants for You, LLP." It took us approximately 2 more years to convince the other associate offices to join us. As Adrian continued to chair the three or four meetings that the partners held annually, we added offices in Ottawa, Montréal, Saskatoon and Toronto to the existing Edmonton and Calgary offices. In 2011, just three months prior to my retirement, Adrian left the DNTW partnership to practice on his own. He continues to do extremely well in Calgary, where he has experienced about a 30% growth in his first year since leaving the national partnership.

In addition to the colleagues I have to thank various people that worked in my office and provided services to our clients. Without their assistance, I would never have had the opportunity to continue my work with the independent contractors.

In my accounting practice, I insisted on using the quality control of having at least two designated accountants review the working papers, financial statements and tax returns for each client. Therefore, I may have gone overboard with the proofreading process for this book as follows:

More directly related to the proofreading of this book, I would like to thank all three of my sons (Mark, Matt and Michael) who gave their time to do just that. Mark and Matt were able to proofread the book from the standpoint of individuals who have considered making the shift from employee to independent contractor. Mike was able to proofread the book from the standpoint of someone who's worked in my office handling the records of independent contractors.

Melissa (Mark's wife) and Leah (Matt's wife) also contributed to the proofreading, from the standpoint of the "so what" approach. I relied on them to primarily watch my grammar and be on the lookout for spelling errors that were overlooked or created by Microsoft.

On the technical side, Graham Wheatley in the Ottawa office of DNTW and Adrian Nagy both proofread the book to ensure that the calculations and comments are technically correct and that I have not overlooked any technical changes that have come into play since my retirement.

Caveat: (I reserve the right to be wrong!)

The author is not a lawyer, nor is he licensed to practice law. The information contained throughout this book is prepared based on research and experience to the date of preparation of the book and is provided strictly for educational purposes. In particular, the draft contract presented in Chapter 13 – The Contractor's Toolbox and all related matters discussed are of a legal nature and the reader is cautioned that they should seek legal advice with respect to the contract and related matters.

Further, accounting and tax laws are subject to change from time to time. The reader should seek appropriate advice from a designated professional accountant that is conversant with the requirements of independent contractors before undertaking the move to operating as a consultant.

CHAPTER 1

When I Grow Up!

Do you recall what you wanted to be when you grow up?

I don't recall what I wanted to be when I was very, very young. In my day, at age five or six most boys wanted to be a policeman or a fireman; perhaps even a cowboy. I don't really know what the girls dreamed of; perchance they wanted to be a ballerina. At eleven or twelve, we became more sophisticated in our goals and perhaps we decided that we would be a private investigator like the "Hardy Boys" or a car mechanic. Some of us might have thought about becoming a doctor, a nurse or even an astronaut.

When it came time to consider what we would be doing after high school or studying at university we also considered occupations like teachers, engineers, accountants, marketers and lawyers. My mother told me, "Whatever you do, do not become an accountant!" (This was likely said at month end as my father, an accountant, was working unpaid overtime.) After two years studying chemical engineering, I gave in and followed the commerce route.

Few adults end up following their childhood dreams. Just as I made the switch from chemical engineering to commerce, many of us change our minds as we get older. Each of my cousins that went to university ended up completing a different course than the one they started with. Even my oldest son Mark began University in the Education program and ended up studying Computer Systems. A small number of us set out to be sales clerks, civil servants, real estate agents or following one of the trades, however that is what many of us ended up doing. There is not anything wrong with following any of these occupations. Most people end up doing something where they generally manufacture, sell, distribute, service, administer or manage in some way.

Where it Starts

At about the age of four or five, we all began a journey of education. It was a journey that would lead us through 15 to 20 years of solid education; all of which was designed to allow us to enter the workforce. We would then be ready to provide our skills, our knowledge and other services to an employer. The education system leads us in most cases to working for a third-party employer. When you look at the above occupations, you will note that almost all the jobs listed are employment of some sort. There is a second form of employment. This other way of being employed is referred to as self-employment or operating your own business. Even into our late teens and early twenties, very few of us look to be self-employed. When we get out of school and start to consider what we really want to do with our lives, it seems that we have a change of heart. The education system provides us with little or no insight into how to handle money. We leave school, knowing very little about money, taxes, debt, putting money aside for investments and virtually nothing about how to raise capital in order to start a business.

In the early 2000's, as I was writing articles for the Edmonton section of the Canadian Information Processing Society's newsletter, I came across a poll prepared by Angus Reid that was conducted on behalf of the Royal Bank of Canada in 2000. Similar results were reconfirmed in about 2005 by the same polling organization. The poll determined that "entrepreneurship is the top career choice of Canadians between 18 and 35 years of age and clearly one-third of Canadians looked to self-employment as how they expected to be earning their living within the ensuing five years."

Now, being an entrepreneur is not exactly the same thing as choosing to be an accountant, a lawyer, a teacher or real estate agent. It is possible that in following any of these occupations, you can be an entrepreneur in some form. Generally when we think of becoming an entrepreneur, we think of setting up some form of large business. The business generally requires a great deal of capital to get underway and often a great deal of "brick-and-mortar." It is often possible to be an entrepreneur in the role of the self-employed individual, as opposed to setting up a full business. Perhaps, at this point we should take a look at how income is earned and types of income that can be earned.

Active versus Passive Income

Active income is earned when we devote our own services (time and skills) to the earning of that income. Passive income is income derived when our personal efforts are not directly required, such as from the earnings of a business or investments.

In our childhood and likely well through our early years of employment, we had little thought of seeking financial freedom. By "financial freedom," I mean being in a position where you do not have to work if you don't want to. Although paper route money I put into savings provided the down payment for our first home, I don't recall starting to look at putting money aside for my future retirement when I started working. About two years after I started working, I met with an insurance agent. This insurance agent advised me that I should be contributing to an RRSP and that I should be doing so on a regular monthly basis. Even being in an articling position as an accountant, it had not occurred to me that this is something I should be looking at, at such an early stage.

Financial freedom is being in a position where you have assets and the income from those assets is sufficient to cover all your ongoing living expenses. I think financial freedom is what we all want to eventually reach. Even if we are not looking to quit working when we retire, we want to be in a position where we may continue to work because we want to, not because we have to work. We do not want to be dependent on providing our services to meet our living costs. We never know when circumstances might arise that will make it impossible for us to continue to earn an active income.

Active Income

Active income is generally derived in one of two ways. The first is through providing our services to an employer for which we receive employment income. The second source of active income is through becoming self-employed and providing our services to one or more clients. Self-employment is generally considered business income. One overriding consideration of earning active income is that it requires the active input of our personal time. Whether the basis for payment is hourly rates, daily rates or a monthly salary, we are remunerated for the amount of time that we spend on behalf of our employer (which may be our own business) or our clients.

This means that we do have a restriction on our ability to earn active income.

One of the constraints of earning active income is realized in that we do not receive the full benefit from our efforts. This shortfall is because we end up paying a number of different types of taxes; income taxes are one of the largest. This is not to say that we don't also pay tax on passive income. It is simply that the taxes on active income are generally much higher.

Active/Passive Hybrid Income

The characteristics of the small business are often difficult to distinguish from that of being self-employed. In a small business, the principal is often involved in providing his or her services on a daily basis and sometimes to a great extent. In this scenario, the individual is more self-employed than operating a business. He or she may receive remuneration as a salary from their own business which clearly makes this active income. The business may earn income well beyond what the principles require to meet their personal living expenses and this is retained in the company and is essentially a passive form of income for the owner.

Characteristics of an Employee

As already mentioned, most people are brought up being trained to get a job as an employee of somebody else's company. Despite the desire of a significant number of Canadians to become an entrepreneur, relatively few follow through. A person who wants to remain as an employee is often afraid to take a risk. They are generally more concerned about the security of their position and possibly the benefits that employment will provide over and beyond the monthly paycheque.

In meeting with potential clients who are looking to make a move from being a full-time employee to become an independent contractor, I would often hear the comment that independent contracting is not as secure as full-time employment. At one time we used to think it was very secure to get a job with an employer and that you would have that job as long as you wanted it. While this is still somewhat the case, if you are a civil servant or working in a unionized position, the last 10 or 15 years have proven that even the major employers can no longer promise you security in your position.

The IT sector in particular went through numerous major layoffs at some of the key companies when the tech bubble burst following Y2K. It is therefore a very big decision for an individual to give up that perceived security of a full-time job to become self-employed. This is predominantly true if they are looking at a potential three or six month contract and knowing that at the end of that time frame, they are going to have to find another contract or perhaps go back to full-time employment.

Monitoring the changes through both good and bad economic times, it is interesting to note throughout my experience in working with a large number of independent contractors, one facet seemed to consistently hold true. That aspect is that it was often the employee who was laid off first, while the independent contractor was retained as long as possible.

As I think back to when I changed jobs early in my career, I was only somewhat concerned I would have a similar benefit package at the new place of employment that I had enjoyed with my previous employer. In each employment change, I was moving from one employer to another and it was not a major concern that they would have reasonable benefits available. For somebody who is moving from being an employee to being an independent contractor, it can be very disconcerting to find that you no longer have a benefit package available to you unless you pay for your own.

When I started working with independent contractors, I was very fortunate to meet with Brenda Douglas of "HDF Financial" in Edmonton. Brenda was the national broker for the Canadian Information Processing Society and a number of the other computer organizations. Through those associations, Brenda has been able to offer insurance and benefit packages designed specifically for the independent contractor. Further, these packages can be obtained at a reasonably modest cost. In many cases, an independent contractor can replace the employment benefit package at a much lower cost than the benefit he was receiving from his previous employer.

If the previous employer was a major Corporation or a government or quasi-government organization, it is also likely that the employer offered a pension plan of sorts. As a self-employed independent contractor, you do not have the benefit of a pension plan paid for by your employer. We do have the ability to contribute to a Registered Retirement Savings Plan to create our own pension.

So it seems that an employee tends to value the perceived security of their position over an opportunity to potentially make more money.

Characteristics of the Self-employed

I am well aware of the characteristic pull within some of us to do things our way. This means we need to operate our own business rather than be employed by someone else. We want to be in control (ownership) of our own destiny. It is difficult for us to work for or sometimes even with others, such as in a partnership. My grandfather and a couple of my uncles operated a sporting goods store in St Catharines, Ontario for over fifty years. Although I had little opportunity to help out in the store, I relished every opportunity I had to do so. I think it may have been this (perhaps inherited) connection that drove me to be self-employed.

While we think of businesses such as the sporting goods enterprise when we consider self-employment, for many this is not a viable objective. Just as I was educated to be an accountant, others are schooled in ways that do not lend themselves to a brick and mortar type of operation. For the doctor, the lawyer, the systems analyst, the engineer, the welder, the real estate agent and many others with service oriented skills, there is the opportunity to be an independent contractor.

Even if you are self-employed, you will be earning active income. Again, this means that you are remunerated for the efforts that you put in with your time. You will still be subject to the relatively high taxes that apply to active income on funds that you withdraw from your business for your personal use. You do gain some tax advantages by being able to deduct the expenses of earning the self-employment income before arriving at the figure on which taxes are calculated. Particularly in the case of a single earner household, the income earned by the self-employed individual can be shared with a spouse commensurate with the effort that the spouse makes towards the operation and success of the self employed business. This allows more of the income to be taxed at lower marginal tax rates.

This book is going to be looking at the segment of self-employed people who provide services rather than selling a product. Some of the clients that came to me discovered self-employment because they were looking for a job. They may have applied for an employment position through a recruiter and that recruiter suggested that perhaps they should consider a position as an independent contractor. They more or less fell into becoming self-employed. The majority of those looking to become independent contractors did so because they wanted some degree of independence and more input on how the work they chose to do would be accomplished.

As with being an employee, when the self-employed individual stops working their income also stops. An employee however may have access to Employment Insurance, which will continue to provide some cash flow for them. A self-employed individual is not permitted to contribute to the government employment insurance plan except for specific benefits. It may therefore be said that a self-employed individual does not own the business; rather they own a job.

It is frequently the professional individual that falls into the self-employed status. They may be accountants or bookkeepers, information technology programmers, or systems analysts, engineers and technologists. Today, there are more and more people who practice one of the construction trades that are also finding self-employment a satisfactory way of earning their living.

While a self-employed individual often has the potential to earn more after-tax income than a full-time employee, they are still subject to the restriction that they have a finite amount of time that could be devoted to their business. In many cases, the person can be satisfied with the differential because it does provide them with the independence and the ability to do things in their own way that self-employment provides. If the self-employed businessman wants to expand beyond his own capabilities, it is important that he learns to benefit from other people's time and/or money. In doing so he can move beyond self-employment and active income to the point where he is receiving passive income through a business and/or through financial investments.

A number of my clients took the step to form a business by hiring subcontractors and benefiting from the revenues that they generated or alternatively banding with other independent contractors. This banding together allowed them to bid on larger projects where they used subcontractors and/or employees to carry out the work. For some contractors, this seems to be a natural progression for them.

You will find in reading through this book, that working as an independent contractor will enable you to earn more after-tax income than continuing the work as a full-time employee. It is extremely important that the cash generated by this additional income is properly managed. For the independent contractor, the investment rather than the consumption of this cash is paramount. This will permit the contractor to begin earning passive income and reach his day of financial freedom much sooner than later.

You should understand that the financial benefits of working as an independent contractor, while significant, are not the only reason why you might want to work in a capacity other than as an employee. The concepts of independent contracting and personal service businesses (PSB) are relatively new in Canada. The PSB rules came about when in the 1960's, Mr. Ralph Sazio, a member of the CFL Hall of Fame and coached the Hamilton Tiger Cats to three Grey Cup championships, redefined his work relationship from employee to incorporated provider, providing control (but not avoidance) of tax payments under significantly higher personal tax rates that were in existence in those days. The federal government took exception to Mr. Sazio achieving tax benefits through incorporation that were not available to him as an employee. This lead to the institution of the PSB rules to make it less attractive to incorporate and provide your services as a consultant rather than as an employee. Recent changes in the PSB rules have gone to extreme making it punitive to be assessed as a personal service business even relative to the tax burden as an employee. It has to make you wonder what today's legislators are thinking! To my mind, the PSB legislation may have made some sense in Mr. Sazio's time. Since then, Canada's economy has changed dramatically. Today's small services business owner/operator is a true entrepreneur that secures work through competitive procurement and competes directly against global corporations for the business that they earn. For many types of knowledge driven work (IT, engineering, technologists and even trades people among others) small business continues to have an advantage over their larger business competitors. This is a tenuous advantage. The PSB legislation reduces the competitiveness of Canada's smaller service businesses and places undue hardships on the owners of those businesses. With the attitude of Revenu Quebec and the Quebec CRA office in going after a number of independent contractors, it is little wonder why Quebec lags well behind the rest of Canada as far as their business competiveness is concerned.

There is an opportunity for Canada. Realizing that a significant number of workers operate as independent contractors and many more would like to, the government can take steps to ensure that the individual working in this manner has a confidence that he will not be assessed after the fact as operating in a manner that was never intended. Taxpayers deserve more certainty in how the tax laws will be applied to them.

Who is this Book For?

I have written this book primarily as a guide for those individuals who have chosen to become self-employed or more so for those who are contemplating making the change from full-time employment to independent contracting as a form of self-employment. The book is aimed at those who earn their income in Canada, rather than from foreign sources. I have not gone into the details of making the transition from self-employment to the point where you operate a self-sustaining business as this exercise could be the subject of a book in and of itself.

I expect this book will be of value to anyone who is contemplating making the change from full-time employment to self-employment. It doesn't really matter whether or not the self-employment consists of providing services or selling a product or some combination of the two. It is aimed more specifically at those who want to operate as an independent contractor in providing personal services to one or more third-parties. The book will also be particularly pertinent to those who are currently operating as independent contractors and will provide some insight into the skills and money management required to be successful.

This book will also be a benefit to anyone who provides services to or for an independent contractor. The book will give you some insight into why people would choose to operate as independent contractors rather than as a full-time employee. Those who would benefit include placement firms, accountants and lawyers. It would be good for these people to understand not only the financial benefits of independent contracting but the many nonfinancial reasons that a person would consider in making a shift in the way they earn their income.

The people who hire employees and/or contractors may be able to understand that there is mutual benefit to be gleaned from embracing the use of independent contractors. Employers, in reading this book, should learn that while they may require a core of employees, there are times when it is better to employ independent contractors.

I do hope that you enjoy reading this book as much as I enjoyed writing it.

CHAPTER 2

The Financial Advantages of Independent Contracting

The Financial Perspective:

While many individuals contemplating independent contracting might be looking to the non-financial aspects of consulting work; as a Chartered Accountant, I have always tended to concentrate on the financial benefits of working as an independent contractor. This is not that I think the other aspects are not pertinent; it is just that independent contracting absolutely blows away full-time employment on a financial basis.

Let me repeat that just for emphasis, "independent contracting absolutely blows away full-time employment on a financial basis!"

Just in case anyone missed it, I want to tell you that there is really no contest at all. From a financial aspect, independent contracting absolutely blows away full-time employment from the perspective of the contractor. I've seen articles written by knowledgeable people in the human resources field and even many by other accountants that tend to claim that the marginal advantage between employment and independent contracting is something in the range of 10% or less. When you're looking at the net after-tax effect I would suggest that it is more like 60% to 80% more after-tax income for the independent contractor as compared to the full-time employee.

What makes it even better is that independent contracting is a financial benefit to both the contractor and to the astute employer that hires the contractor.

I have prepared several scenarios to demonstrate the financial advantage to earning income as an independent contractor. In these examples, we are using 2013 Alberta personal and corporate tax rates. For the examples in this chapter, I have used the Alberta rates because the provincial personal tax component is a flat rate of 10% and the corporate tax rate is a flat 14% throughout the small business income levels. Other provinces use a graduated scale with the effective rate increasing at various levels as taxable income increases. This is similar to the way that federal personal tax rates are structured. In future years the figures will change very slightly as the federal tax brackets are adjusted annually for inflation. At the time of writing, the Canadian inflation rate is negligible.

In order to keep the scenarios simple, I have ignored the effects of Canada Pension Plan (CPP) contributions and employment insurance (EI) contributions. In 2013 the maximum employee CPP contribution is $2,356.20 (Quebec Pension Plan - $2,427.60), which the employer must match. The maximum EI for 2013 paid by the employee is $891.12 ($720.48 – Quebec); the employer must pay 1.4 times ($1,247.52; $1,008.67 in Quebec) as much. The incorporated independent contractor does not pay any Employment Insurance premiums.

A Direct Comparison:

There are three major factors that contribute to the financial advantage that a contractor realizes as compared to his employee counterpart. These factors are as follows:

1. The contractor is generally paid anywhere from 25% to 50% more per hour than the full time employee,
2. The contractor can deduct certain expenses related to earning the income pre-tax while the employee has very few, if any expenses that can be claimed,
3. The contractor may be able to split the income with a spouse or other family member or with his corporation with the result that income is taxed in a lower bracket.

One of the first independent contractor clients I had would tell me he was happy with just the benefit he received from being paid more as an independent contractor than as an employee. He was very reluctant to claim much in the way of expenses, to claim a spouse's salary or pay dividends in lieu of the salary. He wasn't even open to just limiting his salary to the amount of his annual drawings and allowing the excess earnings to be taxed at the low corporate tax rate. He would insist on taking his full corporate net income as a personal salary.

Each year I would provide an analysis for him indicating what his tax savings might be if he were to follow more of my advice in claiming expenses and considering an appropriate salary/dividend split. When he wound up his company about 10 years later, he had accumulated approximately $125,000 in his corporate bank account with a corresponding tax-paid credit payable to him. (How many employees can accumulate this sum after taxes?) While it did serve him well on the company windup that all his tax was paid, his accumulated after-tax earnings could've been so much more.

In the following examples, look at the situations as the same individual working as an employee as compared to him/her working as an independent contractor. This eliminates any consideration of outside factors that might be the case if we compare two separate individuals.

In this first example, we are ignoring the rate advantage used by that particular client, so that we can highlight the benefit derived from the other two factors. We are comparing an employee earning a $100,000 salary against an independent contractor earning the same amount as gross contract income. We have considered the contractor as being married and having the ability to split income with his/her spouse.

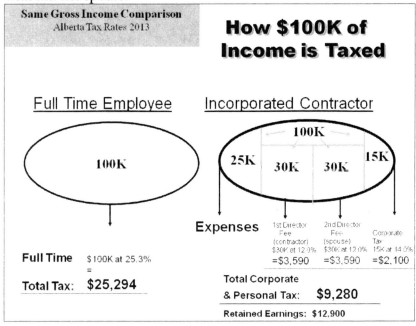

Figure 1: Alta Comparison same

In this scenario, both the employee and the contractor are each paid $100,000 annually for their services. We are assuming that the incorporated contractor incurs $25,000 of annual operating expenses. It is interesting to note that the expenses claimed by an independent contractor are not new expenses for the most part. They are exactly the same expenses that the individual would've paid as a full-time employee. As a full-time employee you have virtually nothing which you can claim against that income aside from some minor tax credits on your personal income tax return. As an independent contractor you are able to claim, with a few specific exceptions, the costs of earning that income. Expenses such as your travel to and from work, some office supplies, a portion of your home including the mortgage interest, some meals and various other expenses can be claimed against your income before any income taxes are calculated. The full-time employee must pay most of these same expenses but they are paid from the employee's after-tax income.

In the diagram, you can see that the employee is paid a salary of $100,000 and pays $25,294 in personal income tax leaving a take-home pay of $74,706. Out of the take-home pay he must still pay about 85% of the expenses ($21,250) that the independent contractor has deducted pre-tax. The employee is therefore left with about $53,456 to use for lifestyle and investment purposes.

On the other hand, the independent contractor and his spouse each pay only $3,590 on their gross salaries of $30,000 and have $26,410 left after the tax (total $52,820) to meet their lifestyle and investment purposes. Plus, the company still has $12,900 left which can also be invested. The contractor therefore has about $65,720 left compared to $53,456 for the employee. **This is a 23.0% increase in after-tax income**.

Summary:

Employee net after taxes and expenses $53,456

Contractor net after taxes and expenses $65,720

Advantage to the contractor $12,264

This advantage arises as a result the second and third factors noted above:

1. First, the contractor is able to deduct certain expenses pre-tax. The nature of the expenses is such that, for the most part, they are the same things that a full-time employee is paying for as well. The expenses include such items as travel from home to the client and back each day, a portion of the home expenses, meals, entertainment and other items. For the

employee these are personal expenses to be paid from his/her after-tax income.

2. Second is the fact that we have a graduated tax scale. As your income increases through the tax brackets, your marginal rate of tax increases. The contractor is able to split income either with a spouse or with his/her corporation. In so doing, more of the income is taxed at a lower marginal tax rate than it would be if earned and taxed in the hands of a single individual.

Consider the long-term advantage that this savings provides over a 25-year career with appropriate cash management. The contractor has $12,264 more per year available than does the employee. Invested at a conservative 2.75% for 25 years this savings would amount to almost $433,000.

The Rate Differential Advantage

In the second example, we show the effect of also adding the rate differential. It is quite typical that an independent contractor will be paid anywhere from 25% to 50% more than a full-time employee doing precisely the same work. This is true because the payor is able to realize various savings such as not having to pay the employer portion of Canada Pension Plan and Employment Insurance premiums, other health, pension, holiday/vacation benefits and training costs, as well as realizing greater efficiency generated from the work of an independent contractor. I like to refer to the independent contractor as "plug-and-play personnel."

In this second scenario, we are comparing an employee making a $75,000 annual salary with an incorporated contractor generating $100,000 of contract income. This is a very realistic scenario. Over the years I had numerous clients with approximately these numbers and this variance between what they had been earning as an employee to what they were now earning in their first contract as an independent contractor.

In the example, the full time employee is paid a salary of $75,000 and pays $16,779 in personal income tax leaving a take home pay of $58,221. As in the first example, out of the take-home pay he must still pay about 85% of the expenses ($21,250) that the independent contractor has deducted pre-tax. The employee is therefore left with about $36,971 to use for lifestyle and investment purposes.

As in the first example, the contractor and his spouse each have $26,410 left from their salaries (total $52,820) to meet their lifestyle and investment purposes plus the company still has $12,900 left which can also be invested. The contractor therefore has about $65,720 left compared to $36,971 for the employee. **With the pay rate differential added, this is 77.8% more after-tax income for the contractor!**

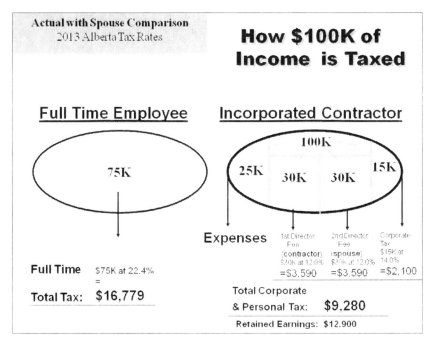

Figure 2: Alta Comparison Full

Summary:
Employee net after taxes and expenses $36,971

Contractor net after taxes and expenses $65,720

Advantage to the contractor $28,749

Again, if we consider the long-term advantage that this savings provides over a 25-year career, we find that the contractor has $28,749 more per year available than does the employee. Invested at 2.75% for 25 years, this savings would amount to about $1,014,400.

What If I Am Not Married or Can't Split Income With My Spouse?

When the contractor is single or has a spouse that works outside the home, it may not be possible or practical for the contractor to fully split the income. Even in one of these situations, there is a significant financial advantage to be an independent contractor as the income can be split with the corporation to take advantage of the low corporate tax rates.

In the following example, the independent contractor draws a higher wage from his/her company as the sole employee.

In this example as in the example above, the full time employee is paid a salary of $75,000 and pays $16,779 in personal income tax leaving a take home pay of $58,221. Out of the take-home pay he must still pay about 85% of the expenses ($21,250) that the independent contractor has deducted pre-tax. The employee is therefore left with about $36,971 and to use for lifestyle and investment purposes.

In order to have the same level of funds in hand as the employee, the individual contractor would take a salary of $44,000 (almost maximizing CPP contributions). The contractor has $37,053 left from his/her salary to meet lifestyle and investment purposes, plus the company still has $26,660 left which can also be invested. The contractor therefore has about $63,713 left compared to $36,971 for the employee. **This is 72.3% more after-tax income for the contractor!**

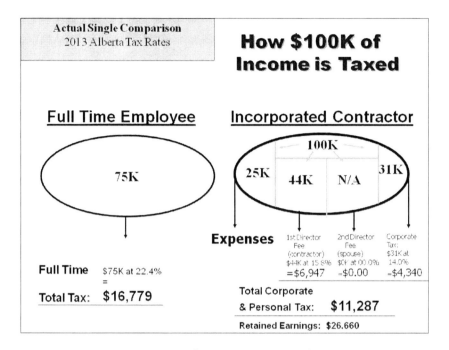

Figure 3: Alta Comparison Single

Summary:

Employee net after taxes and expenses $36,971

Contractor net after taxes and expenses $63,713

Advantage to the contractor $26,742

Once more, if we consider the long-term advantage that this savings provides over a 25-year career, we find that the contractor has $26,742 more per year available than does the employee. Invested at 2.75% for 25 years this savings would amount to almost $944,000.

You will note that in each of these examples, we have paid a salary to the contractor or the contractor and his spouse. In most provinces, there was a distinct tax advantage to paying a dividend or a salary/dividend combination. Doing so generally increased the advantage to the contractor. In the 2013 federal budget, the government has taken steps to eliminate the integration benefit realized by paying dividends rather than a salary. Their objective is to make the tax paid on a dividend equivalent to the tax paid if you take your remuneration as a salary. The politicians have forgotten that a dividend is a return on investment. That is an investment that carries some degree of risk not relevant to a salary. In addition there is a employment tax credit for a salary, but no corresponding credit for dividends. Further, a salary is eligible to create RRSP contribution room while a dividend does not have this privilege. In some provinces, the change in the dividend tax credit will re-introduce double taxation. This will be a major issue for Canadian small businesses regardless whether they are selling services or a product.

In each case demonstrated above, the financial advantage of independent contracting is overwhelming, even using a salary for both, as compared to being an employee.

Proprietorship vs. Corporation

You may have heard somewhere that, "from a financial perspective, independent contracting absolutely blows away full-time employment." We demonstrated this advantage in a comparison of the after-tax incomes earned by an employee and an incorporated independent contractor. Is there still an advantage if the contractor operates as a sole proprietor rather than becoming incorporated?

In Chapter 6 we will compare the various forms in which an independent contractor can operate. From a financial standpoint, there is still an advantage to operating as a proprietorship versus being an employee.

This financial advantage comes about primarily from the first two factors we considered. The contractor is still going to be paid a higher rate versus an employee. The payer still realizes cash savings by employing a contractor instead of an employee and most of this advantage can be passed along to the contractor. The proprietor can still claim the same expenses that are claimed by an incorporated contractor.

Income can still be split with a spouse or other family member; however that may require more day to day input than required with a corporation.

So, you have made the decision to operate as an independent contractor. Is there a difference in the financial opportunity if you operate as a sole proprietor rather than through the use of a corporation?

To answer that question we will look at a comparison of earning gross contract revenue of $100,000 through a proprietorship and through a corporation.

Again, to make the comparison as simple as possible, we will make some assumptions as follows:

1. The gross revenue is $100,000 for both the proprietor and for the corporation. There is no rate differential if you operate either way unless you are contracting through a placement firm. (The placement firm is a special situation where the proprietor is considered a contractor for income tax purposes but an employee for CPP and EI purposes.)
2. Operating expenses total $20,000 of which $3,000 is for meals and entertainment. Such expenses are tax deductible at only 50% of the actual expenditure.
3. The tax rates in effect are those for Alberta 2013. As with the previous examples, we want to use flat rates for simplicity.
4. A salary is taken from the corporation set at $51,100 being the maximum level for 2013 CPP contributions. Please note that the CPP has been removed in the tax calculations below. As the salary for the incorporated contractor is set at the maximum for contributions, there should be no difference in the net tax between the two options.
5. No Registered Retirement Savings Plan contributions (RRSPs) are considered.

	Proprietorship	Corporation
Gross Revenue	$100,000	$100,000
Less:		
Expenses	20,000	20,000
Salary	NIL	51,100
Net Income	$80,000	$28,900
Taxable Income	$81,500	$30,400
TAXES:		
Personal Tax	$18,859	$9,131
Corporate Tax	NIL	4,256
Total Tax	$18,859	$13,387
Net for lifestyle and investments	$61,141	$66,613

Prop Figure 1: Alta comparison with proprietorship table

The sole proprietor reports his net business income in his annual personal tax return and is taxed using the graduated tax brackets. The incorporated contractor can set his salary remuneration at any level required to meet his current lifestyle requirements. It is interesting to note that because the business is now paying for a lot of expenses that would be paid from after-tax income as an employee; a contractor does not require as high a salary as he had as an employee.

The incorporated contractor pays himself a salary of $51,100 and after taxes of $9,131 still has a net of $41,969 from this source. This compares somewhat to the $36,971 retained by the employee ($75,000 salary) after taxes and paying expenses in the earlier examples comparing the employee to the incorporated contractor. In addition, the company still retains $24,644 that can be invested within the company.

In the above table we have used a salary for the incorporated contractor's remuneration rather than a dividend or a salary/dividend combination. Doing so (salary component) would improve the incorporated contractor's position relative to the proprietor in most provinces. Even using a salary for the remuneration, there is still a distinct financial advantage for the incorporated contractor. As the gross and net revenues increase, the discrepancy will grow as more and more of the proprietor's income will be taxed at higher marginal personal tax rates.

In the simple example set out above, the net savings in taxes through a corporation is **$5,472 per year.**

Future Value of $5,472 per annum invested at a rate of 2.75%:

5 years	$ 28,907
10 years	$ 62,013
15 years	$ 99,928
25 years	$193,084

While artificial numbers have been used in the scenarios used here, my "average" incorporated independent contractor client prior to my retirement in 2011 was grossing in excess of $130,000 and spending approximately $19,000 on expenses. The "average" figures are achieved by eliminating the top and bottom 20% of clients and using only the mid–sixty range. I have simplified the figures for illustration purposes. It is true that a corporation will incur higher accounting fees however there may be some expenses that are more difficult to deduct as a sole proprietor than as a corporation. I don't believe the net differences are material to the concept being put forward.

In the schedules section at the end of this book, there are additional comparisons of employee/contractor figures and proprietorship/incorporated contractor for additional provincial tax rates. It is interesting to note that the larger advantages to being an incorporated independent contractor relative to being an employee in the same province is greater in the provinces where the personal tax rates are relatively higher.

CHAPTER 3

Non-Financial Advantages of Independent Contracting

In chapter 2, I indicated that my emphasis was on the financial aspects of independent contracting. I did this partly because of my training and experience as a Chartered Accountant and a Certified Financial Planner. I did it primarily because the financial aspects are so compelling. This is not to say that financial success is assured. In fact, one of my former clients recently declared bankruptcy. For over a decade he had been one of my highest grossing clients. Although his problems stemmed from personal issues, he failed to heed my advice and it caught up to him.

Many times I have listened to my clients tell me that while the financial advantages are nice, it is really the non-financial considerations that they like about the consulting work. This was never more evident than during a meeting with two clients that had both started their contracting careers when I incorporated their companies for them. After a few years of contracting, they had both returned to full time employment because their client had decided that company policy was to use only employees. The contractors had to accept an employment position or look elsewhere for new work. Both of these clients went on at length about the working conditions as employees. They had been faced with doing work that they didn't want to do and were most upset by the office gossip and politics that they would be drawn into. Faced with opportunities to return to contracting, they were in my office to get their corporate records up to date to move forward with their careers in independent contracting. To this day they have not gone back to an employment position.

The Non-financial Advantages

What follows is really only a smattering of the non-financial issues that clients discussed with me over the years. I am sure the list could be twice as long.

Choose projects based on your own career goals, location and personal preferences

This is perhaps the issue that is the most key worthy to "taking ownership of your career." In most employment situations, your employer has a plan for how he will make use of your skills. How you are used and how changes to the way you are directed are decided entirely by your employer.

In my first couple of months as a student–in–training with the Kingston, Ontario office of a National firm, I was called in from doing audit field work that I found very interesting. I felt that I was learning a lot and I was able to apply the new firm standards in flowcharting control systems; a technique in which we had just received training. The time of year was summer and that is the time that the firm went through the annual process of moving the previous years working paper files from the active vaults to a storage room and the contents of the storage room were moved to off-site storage. This was a job that was always assigned to the "newbies."

After a couple of days at this assignment, which was not a pleasant job, the partner I was assigned to was getting anxious for me to get back to the audit work. I passed this information along to the managing partner who was supervising the file movement. He was not at all sympathetic and insisted that I stay at that assignment for at least another day.

That was my introduction to doing what was assigned rather than what would interest me and enhance my career. My son Mark has indicated that at his employment, the contractors may also have to put up with some "crap" jobs as well. This emphasizes that your contract should specify what you are required to do. Be sure to review the comments about contracts in Chapter 8 to be certain that you don't fall into this situation.

For the next seven years, I worked primarily at municipal and other non-profit audits as I got my designation and a promotion to supervisor. Every time I prepared a corporate tax return, it was like I was doing it for the first time. I hardly saw any for-profit clients and that was where my real interests lay. Finally, I asked my supervising partner for a change in assignment. Unfortunately, there were no openings on one of the other partner's teams at that time and it was suggested that I consider a transfer to another office. That is how I came to be in Edmonton! This was in the oil boom of the late 1970s and the Edmonton office was begging for help. I was able to secure a position doing quality control in the small business department. While this gave me the experience that I was looking for at the time and has served me extremely well since, it meant that I had to pack up my young family and move them 2500 miles from friends and relatives.

This unfortunately is what you may have to endure as an employee. You really have little or no say in what assignments you have and where you might be located.

As an independent contractor, you get the chance to select what contracts you want to apply for. If you like to travel, you can pick work that will give you that opportunity or you can stay put in a particular location. You can choose work that is what you want to do and work that will enhance your career goals. Ideally you will move from one contract to the next and they will be exactly what you want to do. Unfortunately, there is not always a suitable contract available when you complete your current contract. To ensure that you can stick to work that meets your career goals and don't have to perhaps take full-time employment or an unsatisfactory contract, it is imperative that you manage your cash to provide a reserve fund. This reserve will allow you to pass on a contract or employment and wait for the work that you really want to do. The financial numbers in the previous chapter indicate that you have a major financial advantage to allow for this wait. It does mean that you must manage your funds appropriately.

Varied work experience without the stigma of frequent job changes

One of the things that an employer looks for when reviewing a resume is a steady and long term employment history. If there are gaps or frequent job changes, an employer will consider that as an unattractive trait. It is very likely that that applicant will never get an interview even though they may have received a great deal of experience in the work they have done over the years. Employment gaps or frequent changes in employment are a bit of a stigma for someone applying for an employment position because an employer is looking for an individual that will be around for a long time. It is a significant financial investment to make when hiring an employee and the employer is looking at your history to find that stability component.

On the other hand, when reviewing the resume of an independent contractor, various changes in employment can actually be a very positive factor. The employer/client will look at it as you having vast experience that can be brought to bear on your contribution to the current project.

A year or two after starting to specialize in services for contractors, I met an individual who had a history of frequent job changes. Every six months or so he would get bored with the work he was doing or the people he was working with and would look for new employment. His wife was a human resources employee. She was the one that suggested to him that he should consider independent contracting rather than continuing as an employee. Her concern was that the frequent changes would be a problem in his resume, but that it might be an advantage as a contractor.

Decide when to work and when not to

As an employee, you are expected to work your daily shift generally five days a week. Depending on the time of year or the particular industry, there may be various alternatives, still directed by the employer. The employer anticipates that you will arrive and leave at designated times. You are allowed certain days off for things like statutory holidays and annual vacations. Again the employer usually dictates when you may go.

As an independent contractor, in most cases it makes a lot of sense for you to work the same hours as your co-workers who are employed. In fact, the employer may specify that he wants you available during those same hours. Unlike with an employee, the employer cannot force you to work those specific hours unless they have been specified in your contract.

NOTE: I would certainly be cautious about having any specific hours noted in a contract. Doing so may be an implication that you are acting more as an employee than an independent contractor. Canada Revenue Agency might seize upon this term as an indication that you are a "personal service business" rather than an independent contractor despite the existence of the contract. An in depth discussion of this is looked at in Chapter 8.

While an employee needs employer approval to arrive late or leave early, the contractor may find he needs to do things of a personal nature or for his own business (e.g. meet with his accountant). He does not need the client's permission to leave work to carry out these tasks. I do caution that it would still be appropriate to ensure that all matters requiring your attention have been dealt with before you leave.

An employer expects an employee to be chained to his desk until quitting time. The employee is being paid for that time. A contractor may leave at any time if the day's work is complete. He only invoices for the hours that he actually works.

Beyond the daily hours, there are other times that you might want to be away. I had several clients that had worked for the government and received their gold-plated pension at the ripe old age of 55. They were not ready to stop working but didn't want to work full time. They would go down south during the cold winter months and return in the spring to pick up roughly a six month contract which would allow them to return to warmer climes the next winter. These clients found that the independent contractor lifestyle worked very well for them. It allowed them the ability to take advantage of an early retirement, yet they were able to continue to keep their hand in and remain in the social circle they had become accustomed to.

With the prospect of the baby boom generation leaving the workforce en mass in the coming decade, perhaps a taste of independent contracting would allow those who would like to slow down but not quit, the opportunity to keep making a meaningful contribution. This can be beneficial to both the individual and the employer who will soon find an experienced workforce difficult to find.

Gain new experience and knowledge

An individual who works for a long time doing basically the same thing day after day will become very good at his job. As things change in the way things are done, he will have the opportunity to learn new ways to accomplish the same work he has been doing. If he is astute, he will also absorb information from the things that go on around him and from the people that he works with. All in all though, new experiences and gaining significant new knowledge will be relatively minimal. Employers see an employee who is very good at what they do and they want to keep them doing that same function. After a while, you become bored and really stop learning.

It was a desire for a change in what I was doing that brought me to Alberta from Ontario. Saddled with municipal and non-profit work for seven years, I wanted to get more experience with small business. My transfer to the small business department and doing quality control work was a combination of factors that I feel honed my knowledge of business and furthered my skills in maintaining high quality in all that I have been associated with since. Even with these benefits, I missed the direct contact with the clients. To regain that contact, I needed to move on.

Many years later, it was a further desire to change the work I was doing that led me to specialize in working with independent contractors. When I began this work, I researched everything I could to become knowledgeable about the needs of the contractor. I began writing newsletter articles for the Canadian Information Processing Society's (CIPS) newsletter in Edmonton and then started delivering seminars. All this was a new experience for me. None of it would have been possible if I had remained an employee. Being self-employed allowed me the latitude to explore new avenues.

Control the development of your skill set and direction of your career

As noted above, an employer will pigeon hole an employee when they find they are capable of doing some one thing particularly well. From that point on it is the employer that has ownership of your career. What you want to do and what you want to be involved in take second place to the desires of the employer.

As a contractor, you have the opportunity to select contracts that will allow you to do the type of work that you want to do. It is imperative that you manage your cash well so that you are in a position when looking for a new contract to be able to wait for a contract that will meet your criteria. Many employers still think that they are in control in an interview. You need to be sure that you are the one in control. Don't be afraid to be tenacious in seeking out exactly what you will be required to do. Don't settle if it will not further what you want to do.

Make connections in various industries

You may be able to work in various industries. Particularly for the information technology contractors, the skills in one industry carry over to many others. Having experience in various industries may make it easier to find the contract work you are looking for when economic times are tougher. If one economic sector is experiencing difficulties, another industry may still be looking for the skills that you possess.

For others, a particular niche may be more desirable. Just as I found that being the expert for independent contractors was a better way to build a large clientele, you may want to be the expert in a small market. If you are recognized as having a particular skill or knowledge, it makes you much more marketable in that sector.

Develop soft skills (high demand) you will use in other facets of your life

The need to set up your own operation and take on the responsibility of ensuring that you have consistent work provides you with on the job training in the people skills that are so sought after by employers. If there is a choice between two equally qualified candidates from a technical standpoint, the individual with the better people skills will get the nod.

Just as we speak of the bedside manner of a doctor, it is important for an independent contractor to also be able to speak and listen and assess such that others are prepared to reciprocate. I once worked with a Chartered Accountant that was brilliant technically but could not translate that to the clients. You must develop the soft skills if you want to succeed as an independent contractor.

The soft skills will help you in other facets of your life. While it is well known that most people would rather be in the coffin than delivering the eulogy at a funeral, the requirements of being an independent contractor will permit you to gain experience and self-confidence to stand up and make that speech. It is a useful skill in many situations.

Escape from office politics

This is the benefit that I hear most often from contractors. It is almost impossible to avoid dealing with office politics. I always found as an employee that office politics was the main topic that stretched from gossip to watching your back. Office politics is very draining on employee productivity and next to absenteeism is probably one of the greatest inefficiencies in the workplace today. In fact; absenteeism is very frequently a symptom of "office politics." The mentally draining effect of office politics can cause an employee to become so mentally fatigued that they become physically or mentally ill and simply cannot face going in to work.

For the independent contractor, the effect of office politics is minimized. Being paid to fulfill a specific function for a specified period of time, you don't have to be concerned with who gets promoted over whom. You don't have to be concerned with who is seeing who after hours or in the stairwell. You don't have to be concerned with what corporate strategy the company is following. You don't have to listen to the latest gossip. You get paid for the work that you produce and so you keep your head down and do just that. It results in considerably less mental strain than what you go through as an employee.

Since office politics is such a drain on productivity, it is also one of the major reasons that many employers are quite ready to hire independent contractors to fill out their roster.

Earn income directly proportionate to your contribution

Being a conservative capitalist at heart, I believe that being remunerated based on your own efforts rather than on a set pay scale is a huge reward in itself! As a new contractor, you may still have to accept what is being offered, but you do have the right to refuse the work if it doesn't meet your requirements.

Most contractors are paid on an hourly basis at a specified rate. If you put in more hours in a day than standard, you may be able to complete your project in less time than expected. This may also be true if because of your abilities you are able to work faster than others, you will have the same result. This will give you the remuneration you expected from your contract and it will allow you to move to your next contract sooner than anticipated. This allows you to earn your remuneration proportionate to your input of skills and effort.

Develop your entrepreneurial skills

As an independent contractor, you must learn to market your skills through negotiating the terms of your contract. You will be required to maintain adequate accounting and banking records and be able to produce them for your accountant on a timely basis. You will learn how to hone your skills and be on the lookout for changing requirements. Through all of this you will also learn to manage your relationships with suppliers and co-workers. You may have the opportunity to make presentations to your clients directly or on their behalf to their clients.

All of the above events will put you in good stead for operating not only your independent contracting business, but any business that you want to operate. Entrepreneurial skills are not taught in schools. You can take courses in management functions, but none of them teach you what needs to be done in the moment. That is something that is learned only through experience. I will be the first to admit that I made some mistakes along the way. I believe that I learned from those errors and it stood me in good stead. As an independent contractor you will be exposed to all facets of operating a business of your own and you will have the opportunity to develop those skills as you go.

★ ★ ★ ★ ★

Times You Should Be an Employee

If both the financial aspects and non-financial aspects are so good, why would anyone ever accept full-time employment?

Contracts are short term

In many cases, an initial contract may be for only a three month term. Most contracts in Information Technology run six months to a year. In engineering, the contracts may be as long as three years as a project can often last for an extended length of time. In many of the trades the contracts may be seasonal or for less than a year at a time. The length of the contract is somewhat dependent on the type of project that you are assigned to and somewhat related to the economic and/or technological viability of that project.

Although the initial short term contract is generally extended, you may find yourself looking for a new job in a relatively short period of time. Depending on the economic activity at the time this may a challenge.

An independent contractor will generally make as much after-tax in eight months as a full time employee will in a full year of employment. Financially, a little down time should not hurt you. You should anticipate and plan for unexpected down times. If you however, are not mentally able to accept that there will be times when you are out of work or frequent times when you have to find new work, you might be better off to find full-time employment rather than consider contracting.

Having said that, I have seen many instances where employees have been laid off before the contactors were let go during bleak economic times.

Employment is the only game in town

Just as many individuals discover independent contracting because a consulting position is the only match for their skills when looking for work, there will be times when no contracts are available (at least none that you want). I have always encouraged my clients to manage their cash such that they have a reserve that will allow them to wait for the contract that suits them. If they have that reserve, they are able to sit and be choosy about the work they want to do.

If they don't have that reserve, they may be forced to accept an employment position for the short run. It is better to have some income coming in than nothing. Otherwise, the bills will pile up and you will be starting in a big hole when you do get a contract.

For training or to learn new skills

This is perhaps the most legitimate reason to accept an employment position and is still a sign that you are taking ownership of your career. As an independent contractor, you are responsible for your own training. You are expected to be a "plug and play" individual. If a client were to pay for your training, you might be considered to be an employee by Canada Revenue Agency and they will assess you as a "personal service business." This assessment would result in many expenses being disallowed and being taxed at the top corporate tax rates rather than at the small business tax rates.

An independent contractor may be able to take courses to learn new skills. There is a high cost to obtain this knowledge. You will have unpaid downtime, the cost of the course/training, and possibly travel, meals and accommodation costs as well. If these skills are simply to compliment the current skill set, the courses may enhance your marketability. In most cases however, the employer will want to know what you have done with the knowledge learned and less with what knowledge you have obtained.

On the other hand, if you were to take an employment position, the employer would likely pay you while you are receiving the training. He would also bear the costs of the training which include the registration/tuition fees and the costs related to attendance at the training course. (The cost of a full time position may be greater than paying these costs yourself.) Once the knowledge/skills have been learned the employer will most likely put you in a position to make use of the new skills. When you return to the contractor marketplace, you will have both the knowledge and the experience using that knowledge. You will definitely be more marketable and may also command a higher rate.

I do caution that you might want to get the employer to commit to the training and the experience in writing. I had a few clients that went to employment and never got the training they had been promised or if they did get the training, they were never given the opportunity to apply that knowledge and get the experience in using it.

I suggest that if you do find yourself in a position where you must fall back on full-time employment that you simply consider it to be another contract (albeit a low paying one) and that you keep your eyes out for another contracting position that meets your interest and skill criteria. Also if you take a full-time position, you should be prepared to work at it for a reasonable period of time. I suggest about six months is adequate if you are forced into the position and at least a year if you have made the move to get training and specific experience. I look at the shorter time for the position where they insist on employment rather than contracting as the employer is really not doing you much of a favour. On the other hand, you never want to burn your bridges with a potential client/employer.

CHAPTER 4

Employer Advantages of Contractors

The Mutual Benefit:

When we looked at the first scenario in Chapter 2 Financial Advantages of Contracting, we compared an employee grossing a salary of $100,000 and a contractor grossing the same amount. The advantage to the contractor, while not startling, was still very significant.

The advantage in this scenario came about as a result of two factors:

1. First, is the detail that the contractor is able to deduct certain expenses pre-tax. This is essentially a way to legally avoid tax. The claiming of the expenses reduces the taxable income so that no tax will be paid on the income that is offset by the expense deduction. The nature of the expenses being claimed by a contractor is such that, for the most part, the deducted expenses are the same expenditures that a full-time employee is required to make, but cannot claim against income. The employee therefore must pay these same expenses with his after-tax income. The expenses include such items as travel from home to the employer/client and back each day, a por-

tion of the home expenses, meals, entertainment and other items. For the employee these are personal expenses to be paid from his/her after-tax income.

2. Second is the fact that we have a graduated tax scale. As your income increases through the tax brackets, your marginal rate of tax increases. The contractor is generally able to split income either with a spouse (commensurate with the work the spouse has done on behalf or for the benefit of the business) or with his/her corporation. The ability to split income is a tax savings. With at least a portion of the income taxed in a lower marginal tax bracket, there is a permanent tax savings. In so doing, more of the income is taxed at a lower tax rate than it would be if earned and taxed in the hands of a single individual.

The above factors allow the independent contractor to realize a significant increase in the amount of after-tax income as compared to his/her full-time employed counterpart. There is yet another factor to consider. It is this third factor that also makes it beneficial for the employer to hire contractors as opposed to employees.

The third factor is that a contractor will generally be paid anywhere from 25% to 50% more than a full time employee doing the same work. We brought this factor into the second and third scenarios in Chapter 2. This factor makes a perceptible difference in the financial advantage of being an independent contractor.

You might wonder why an employer would ever consider hiring an independent contractor if he has to pay him 25% to 50% more than an employee to do the same work! This is the real beauty of independent contracting! Despite paying more per hour for a contractor, there are benefits realized and cost savings realized that allow the employer to do this and still come out ahead as well.

Employers can pay this level of premium and still find contractors to be more efficient and cost effective despite these higher hourly rates for the following reasons:

Efficiency: A study of the use of contractors in the late 1990s leading up to the turn of the century was reported in what was called *"The Year 2000 Study."* This study reported that "the virtual workforce is 17% more productive and significantly more cost effective, than permanent or career employees." Much of this productivity gain results from the fact that the independent consultant does not have to deal with social and political distractions present in most places of employment. The independent contractor is generally an enthusiastic, incentive-driven worker.

Many of my clients, particularly those who had tasted contracting and then returned to employment, were very adamant that the office politics were very distracting as an employee. Several indicated that getting away from this distraction was one of the primary reasons they were returning to contracting.

I am aware that at one employer in the information technology field, one of the senior bosses was asked to find other employment. This happened early one morning and productive work by all the employees on his team stopped as soon as the word was out. Upper management spent time discussing the transition with them and then the entire team was allowed to take part of the day off with pay. Meanwhile, the contractors working beside them remained at their post throughout the day continuing to produce.

No Benefit Package: Productivity (efficiency) may be a hard thing to measure without some expert skills in that particular field. More concrete figures come when looking at the overall benefit package and at the cost saving to the employer that comes with writing a cheque. When a contractor receives that additional hourly pay, it is not like there is no trade-off for the contractor. The independent contractor will not be paid annual holidays, statutory holidays, sick days and any overtime will likely be at straight time as laid out in the contract. There are other benefits that an employee may receive that will not (and should not) be extended to a contractor.

Hiring contractors eliminates, for the employer, many of the most often overlooked costs of employees: benefits and payroll taxes, pension plans and their administration costs, not to mention the various downtime days as noted above! According to the Canadian Payroll Association, businesses can save about 28 percent (on average) of their payroll costs by contracting out; about 18 percent by not paying benefits and about 10 percent by not paying payroll taxes. A "KPMG" study in the early 2000s found the savings to be about 41% for upper level personnel.

It is generally harder to let an employee go because of a requirement to pay a severance fee on their termination. This can amount to a significant figure for long term employees. It is a severe penalty on the employer (getting nothing in return) to get rid of an employee that is no longer considered to be contributing to the goals of the organization. On the other hand, most contracts with independent contractors provide for a very short termination and no requirement to pay a severance fee.

I have been told by many employers that contractors are too expensive and that it costs too much to hire one as compared to an employee. This same tale has been repeated numerous times by contractors being let go because the employer says they cost so much more than an employee. If one were to look at the monthly cheque going to the contractor and compare it to the monthly pay cheque going to an employee, the contractor's cheque would undoubtedly be much higher. If you then consider that with an employee, there is a second cheque going to Canada Revenue Agency for source deductions, a third cheque going to an insurance provider for a health benefit plan and possibly a fourth cheque going to a pension administrator, plus various other benefits paid along the way such as transit passes or parking. Add up all of these cheques and then compare the total to the amount of the single cheque going to the contractor. Although each employment situation is unique, I have little doubt that the multiple cheques will total to more than the amount being paid to the independent contractor.

When comparing the cheques above, you would also need to note that the cheque to the employee may be paying for time for which no work was accomplished. On the other hand, the cheque to the contractor is all for work actually done.

One of the daily newspapers in Edmonton, Alberta used to have a columnist who was assigned to the City Hall beat. Every year when the city budget was being debated, this columnist would prattle on about the high cost of consultants. I felt it was my duty to send him an e-mail and explain that consultants are actually a financial benefit to the city. However, I received no response from him. This columnist left the paper to successfully run for a position on city Council. Now, when the city budget is being debated he continues to berate the city's administrative staff over the extensive use of consultants. He states that the current city employees should be doing the work that has been assigned to consultants.

I continually wonder what the city employees must be doing currently if they can suddenly be reassigned to special projects. If they are reassigned, who is going to be doing the work that they are currently doing today? In most cases the work that consultants are hired for is project based or may require a specific set of skills that may not be readily available in-house. I suppose the city could spend money to educate an in-house employee so that they then had these particular skills however, that would probably be for a one time use and for a limited period of time. All of this seems to me to be highly inefficient use of your current staff and I remain surprised that someone would even suggest this.

You cannot simply look at the amount being paid to contractors/consultants and say that this is too much money. You also have to consider what the actual cost would be to use current employees or alternatively to hire additional employees in lieu of hiring consultants.

No Training Costs: When I have interviewed prospective clients considering the move to independent contracting, one of the things they often mention is the ability to obtain training courses fully paid for by their employer. They now realize that, as an independent contractor, they will be responsible for funding their own training costs. Often I have asked a contractor who has made the choice to return to full-time employment after a period of working as an independent contractor, why they've made that decision. The answer I frequently got is that they are looking to acquire a skill in a particular area, and they feel that they will get the training and hands-on experience as a full-time employee more readily than if they undertook the training themselves.

A contractor can generally find a course or an education program that will provide him with the necessary knowledge to perform a particular skill. The problem with this situation is that it is unlikely that he will have the hands on experience to go with the education. As "plug–and–play personnel," an independent contractor needs the corresponding experience on his resume to convince a particular client that he is capable of fulfilling the contract in an efficient and competent manner.

For the employer however, tuition, transportation, accommodation and downtime are considerable training expenses to be paid on behalf of an employee.

On the other hand, the contractor generally requires a minimal amount of training as he or she is being hired for a particular set of skills that he or she can demonstrate competency in.

Project Based Staffing: Much of high tech/high skilled work is project based and as such requires specific skills for a limited amount of time. A contractor is paid only for the work they do while a permanent employee must still be paid during slow periods and for downtime functions. Hiring contractors minimizes the enormous cost of searching for and hiring each employee. If the skills required are predominantly specific, it is unlikely that a current employee will be competent in that skill, especially if he has not been currently using the skill involved.

Through the use of independent contractors, the cost of downsizing can be mitigated as well when a project is completed or manpower requirements decrease. It can be expensive to lay off an employee, but most consulting contracts have a termination clause with no costs attached.

Pool of Talent: Contract staff can be hired for particular skills and they will devote their time to the application required. Employees must be kept productive. Even if you have the individual with the proper skills on staff, it may be questionable whether or not they are available when their skills are required.

As with the previous concerns about the Edmonton city budget, the city managers would need to be concerned whether or not their current staff had the particular skill set that is required for the particular project. If an individual did have the skill set required, would they be available to work on the new project without disrupting his or her current work schedule and commitments? The particular skill set may be required for only a limited period of time. So what would the city do with that particular employee when his usefulness on the new project terminates? That employee may very well be relegated to "sitting on the bench" at a significant cost. Through the use of an independent contractor, this cost can be avoided as the contract may be terminated with the termination of the project.

Why Employers Love Contractors:

Essentially, hiring an employee is a million-dollar decision, while hiring a contractor is a $65 per hour decision. As a former employer, I can assure you that your staff can make your whole day enjoyable or it can be hell!

To hire an employee one must go through many steps just to get a likely candidate in the door. You will likely have to provide a bevy of benefits to attract them to work with you. It takes some time to get them up to speed during which they are somewhat unproductive, yet earning full wages. Once they are productive you need to keep them off the bench and productive in order to earn from their efforts. If you find they are not the solution you were looking for, you will have to let them go and likely will have to pay a severance (a really stupid concept) that gives them more remuneration for no work.

If you happen to hit the jackpot by finding an efficient long term employee, then you are indeed fortunate and that will work to your benefit. Every company needs a core of full time employees that will provide continuity for you and for your clients.

Over the years, I made some really good hires, however I also had some real poor choices. I can only recall a period of about 18 consecutive months when I was really happy with all my employees. In my accounting firm, I found that it takes at least six months for even the best and experienced employees to become productive and start earning the way we hope they will. If at the end of those six months, they didn't cut it, I found I was out the guarantee that any placement firm would provide and I was back to interviews and another six month break in period.

Obviously, it is expensive to make a bad hire.

On the other hand, hiring an independent contractor is not as great a risk. First, you are hiring a "plug and play" person. They are expected to have the skills to come in and do the job unsupervised in a short period of time. Second, if they don't work out, you can generally let them go with only a couple of days notice and no severance requirements. Presumably, they have been somewhat productive and you have only paid them for the work they have done to date. You received some benefit for the money paid out.

Flexibility is a key advantage of using independent contractors. Having owned and operated a business that was swamped for about four months of the year and struggled sometimes to keep busy the other eight, I know very well that hitting the right level of staffing can be critical. You need staff with requisite skills at specific times to meet the needs of your clients, yet you can't have so many people that they spend much of their time just trying to look busy. That has to be the hardest job around!

Even after smoothing our annual workflow somewhat by encouraging my clients to select fiscal year ends that would spread our corporate work to those eight "slower" months, I often compared the workflow through the office to a snake swallowing a frog. We still had times when we had numerous fiscal year ends and the files would pile up faster than my technicians could handle them. At the same time, the reviewers and I were comfortable with our workloads. The technicians would put in extra time and soon they would be getting caught up with the files. At that point, my reviewers would be feeling the pinch with a backlog of files waiting for their attention. When the reviews were caught up, it would fall to me and I would be swamped with meetings to review the financial statements with the clients. Then the files would move on to my secretary who would print and assemble the statements and returns and set appointments for clients to come in to sign the returns. Hopefully, the analogy ended before the results came out at the end.

Although my technicians were all employees, I was fortunate that my wife was quite competent in preparing personal (T1) tax returns, and the returns to report client's (T4) annual payroll and source deduction remittances and to report (T5) dividends paid. The T4 and T5 returns were prepared in January and February each year with a due date at the end of February. The T1 returns were prepared in March and April and were due at the end of April. The fact that she managed these returns and prepared most of them herself allowed the other technicians to concentrate on completing the corporate fiscal year ends and so we were able to smooth the months in which we were swamped by using a temporary employee. In fact Linda worked more like a contractor coming in to do my own records and to cover off on secretarial duties whenever we had a changeover.

I was also fortunate that when one of my best technicians had to move away for family reasons, he continued to work remotely for me as a contractor. Although he maintained full time employment elsewhere, we were able to increase and decrease his workload as we hit peaks and valleys in our files on hand.

At the reviewer level, both of my reviewers were contractors running their own small practices and able to step in to meet the excess workflow as it passed through that step in the process. Unfortunately, there was no one to replace me. I simply had to work more hours; generally 2400 to 2600 annually. I was able to use the reviewers (both designated accountants) to do tax research and special calculations (e.g. capital dividend account determinations) that I couldn't find the time for myself.

The point here is that project work and periodic (sometimes temporary) periods of increased work can be met with the use of hiring a contractor. As soon as the need for the extra staffing passes, the contractors can move on to other work. If the influx of work was solved by hiring permanent staff, the employer would be faced with underemployed people when volumes returned to normal or they would be looking at layoffs with all the inherent problems that brings.

Major layoffs in a public company signal a potential problem drawing unwarranted media attention and possible market value considerations whereas not renewing contractors is a normal business occurrence.

Independent contractors allow the employer to meet workload fluctuations; both increases and decreases in an orderly manner at minimal cost.

Similar results can happen when the employer requires special skills for a specific job or time frame rather than to smooth workloads. Sometimes it is not the workload that is a problem for an employer. It could be that short term or temporary requirement of someone that that has a specific skill that is not readily available from the normal workforce. This is again an issue that we come across frequently in the accounting profession. A sole practitioner or indeed any small firm cannot be all things to all clients. A sole practitioner will often have to consult with an independent tax consultant when a client needs specialized or more sophisticated tax advice than the practitioner is prepared to offer.

I suspect that this is a concern that comes up fairly often with most corporations. For example; when the City of Edmonton undertakes a transportation project with respect to light rail transit, they may have many employees that are familiar with issues related to road construction or bus transportation. It is not likely that they would have the required skills/knowledge to translate that to the light rail system or a specific portion of that project. True, they could find and employ an individual or spend the time and money to train a current employee. What if however, that person is only required for a short time frame? What if that specific skill/knowledge is only required for six months or a year? What do you do with the employee you hired specifically for this job? If you were to train a current employee, how long would it take and would that employee now have training but no real experience? It would often make sense to find someone with the required skill/knowledge that already has relevant experience and hire them on a contract basis rather than as an employee!

Specialization of skills can increase productivity such that the job can be completed in less time and much more efficiently than if full time employees are utilized. An individual that has been doing certain work for some time ought to be much more efficient at completing it than a individual that only handles it on occasion.

In my early years in accounting, I handled mostly municipal and non-profit work. When I was faced with drafting a corporate tax return, it was so rare that each time seemed like the first time. It required me to act slowly and methodically to ensure that I got it complete and accurate. Once I moved to Edmonton and started reviewing five or six returns a day, I got to the point where I could complete a full return in less time and with more confidence than it used to take to complete the client's name and address.

In my situation I was an employee rather than a contractor, however the example does underline the issue that using people that have experience and knowledge in a certain area is better than trying to fit someone to a situation. Using independent contractors to handle specific issues on a major project is often more productive than getting an employee up to speed. This is yet another reason that an employer would prefer to use an independent contractor than employee. It results in a saving of time and money that does not reflect in the pay cheques.

Contracting costs have been shown to be much less than hiring an employee to do the same work. We have already talked about the hidden costs of an employee. These are the direct costs that don't get included in the pay cheque but are employee related. The source deductions, benefits and down time for holidays, vacations, sick days and no work available days are just some of the extras that an employer has to handle with an employee. An independent contractor may also want a vacation and will from time to time call in sick. In these situations, the employer may get behind in a project (as he would with an employee as well) but he doesn't otherwise have to pay out of pocket. With a contractor, if no work is being done, there is nothing to be paid out.

We have also seen that beyond the physical payment of money, there are ways in which an independent contractor can be more effective and efficient than a full time employee. The productivity gained from a separation from office politics and other issues and the efficiency gained by applying specific skills for a determined amount of time can make using a contractor very cost efficient for an organization. An astute employer should be on the lookout for opportunities to make use of contractors rather than adding another full time employee.

Ease of termination is a major consideration for employers. As most contractors are hired for specific skills or for project work it is easy to terminate the contract when the project ends or is completed or when the specific skills proffered are no longer required. Most contracts should have an end date. If the services are required beyond that end date it is relatively easy to renew the contract or to provide an extension to it. On the other hand, if a project terminates prior to the end of the contract, or if the work of the contractor proves unsatisfactory, it is likely that the contract has a term that allows the employer to cancel it with relatively little notice. In such cases, both parties part ways and there are no further issues to deal with.

If for economic or other reasons an employee's services are no longer required, it is much more difficult to terminate them. This is particularly true if the employee has been around for a substantial period of time. Arrangements may have to be made for transfer or even the payout of of pension plans or benefit entitlements. Many employees will be eligible for a severance payment which is a payment for no work and no production.

The ease with which contractors can be moved into and out of an organization is something that makes an independent contractor very attractive to an employer.

Reducing workload pressure on core staff is perhaps the best use of an independent contractor and one of the greatest benefits for the employer. I concur that it is imperative for virtually any organization to have a core of employees. I also believe that this core is better served if they are supplemented from time to time by the use of independent contractors to help out as a company goes through a strong growth period or when it has seasonal or economic speed bumps. It can really hurt morale and affect personal and corporate health if some of your employees are required to put in excessive hours periodically.

I often found that my staff and I had to work extremely hard for a long period of time before it became economically possible to make another hire. The insertion of an independent contractor can ease the step to the next level.

★ ★ ★ ★ ★

Some Myths Put Forward by Employers

Limited time to be a contractor with one employer: Over the many years that I was immersed in providing the accounting and tax services to independent contractors, there were certain organizations that would really embrace the hiring of independent contractors. After period of time, I would meet with one or more contractors that had been employed at one of these good locations and they would inform me that a new manager is now in place and the organization is moving to an employee only status. The contractor's currently in place are being offered at least an option to become full-time employees. When it comes time for contract renewal, in many cases, the individual is told that he must become a full-time employee, or there will not be ongoing work for him.

This is an indication that a new manager has been hired that does not understand the financial benefit to his company and the many related benefits that go with having a staff beyond the core staff that make up their workforce. I believe that most of the commentary above should put this concern to rest. If not, hopefully a contractor will make a gift of this book to that particular manager to perhaps enlighten him to the benefits of using contract staff. With any luck, he will understand that a failure to use such staff is actually costing his company money.

In the earlier years of working with independent contractors; many who had worked at IBM would indicate when their contract came up for renewal that the company insisted that using a contractor for a period of more than two years would dictate that the contractor was a personal service business rather than an independent contractor. As will be discussed in Chapter 8, where we look at the risks of operating as an independent contractor, we will find that to be declared as a personal service business requires the subjective weighting of a whole multitude of individual criteria. A two-year timeframe is not a defined cut off point; however an extended contract is one of the many criteria that are considered. Just because a situation where a series of contracts have been extended for two or more years has occurred, it does not mean that the consultant is a personal service business.

I don't know how IBM arrived at this criterion. I suspect that they got burned by Canada Revenue Agency at some point. There would certainly have to be more criteria involved in the particular situation than an extended contract. Even the upper tax courts in recent years have indicated that the length of time that a contractor works for a particular client is not a consideration that carries much weight. It really depends much more on the particulars of how the relationship is managed and with what the intention of the parties involved is.

A recent Quebec tax case established that the length of time working with one client is not a factor when considering whether or not a company is engaged in a personal service business rather than operating as an independent contractor. Although this case will not be a precedent in the rest of Canada, it will be a consideration for the federal courts to reconcile with.

Generally speaking, a contractor should not be overly concerned if he is repeatedly renewed or hired for new contracts by the same client over an extended period of time.

It costs too much to hire a contractor:
A frequent myth put forward by many employers is the relative cost of hiring a contractor versus cost of hiring an employee. I believe we have sufficiently discussed this issue in preceding paragraphs. I would hope that any employer reading this book will now go back and provide a full analysis of the cost of hiring and perhaps even firing an employee versus the cost of using an independent contractor.

Employees will stay longer than contractors:
One of the more unique excuses for not using contractors is that they're more likely to move on to new employment than a full-time employee. My experience with my clients would indicate this is not the case. If an employee is not happy in the work they are doing or are not satisfied with their level of remuneration, I think they are more likely to make an employment change. That is, the contractor who has specifically taken on the work he is doing and is effectively earning much more than the full-time employee will be more likely to be satisfied with his situation. Also, my clients have frequently indicated they would be quite happy to stay on and continue to do the work they are doing but they are not prepared to accept a lower pay, or perhaps be reassigned to other work they are not interested in.

So when you consider these factors, it is more likely that an employee will move on before an independent contractor will.

Marginal differences in rates offered.

In previous chapters, we indicated that an independent contractor can expect to be paid between 25% and 50% more per hour than a full time employee. There are many instances however where my clients have indicated very marginal differences being offered. In some cases this difference is between $2 and $5 on contracts that range from a low of $25 per hour to about $70 per hour. I suggest that the employers in these situations may not yet understand the benefits they are realizing by using independent contractors.

In the case of the lower rate contracts, the option may be term employment with no benefits. In this case, the low margins between contracting and employment may be called for. The individual considering this option should consider whether or not he/she wants to make a career as a contractor. If so, the contracting option may be a way to get your first contract. Second and more lucrative contracts may follow as future employers will look at you as an experienced contractor.

The higher rate contracts are a different matter. Contracts over $35 an hour seldom compare to term employment. Full employee benefits are generally the norm for the employee alternative. As such, the employer will gain the contractor cost savings including source deductions, health and other benefits, pension costs and down time savings. In addition, there are the productivity benefits that accrue to the employer and the overall organization. The $5 differential being offered is covered pretty much by the source deduction savings alone.

An interesting issue comes up with a sole proprietor contracting through a placement firm. This is a special situation where the individual is considered an independent contractor for income tax purposes but is considered to be an employee for purposes of Canada Pension (CPP) and Employment Insurance (EI). In this situation, the placement firm must withhold and remit CPP and EI from the individual and remit it together with the appropriate employer portion on a regular basis. The contractor should be aware that he is going to be paying the cost for this tax one way or another. In a few instances, the placement firm will charge an "administration" fee which happens to work out to the amount of the employer portion of CPP and EI being remitted each month. More often, the placement firm will offer you an alternative rate for your contract. You will get a higher hourly rate if you are incorporated as the placement firm does not have to administer the withholding and remittance of the source deductions.

Summary:

It is quite evident that the benefits of using independent contractors in the workforce can be advantageous to the employer as well as the employee. Employers should be encouraged to look for opportunities to use contractors/consultants to supplement the core workforce whether it is to smooth out the ups and downs of the workflow or to seek out specific skills that are not otherwise readily available. In doing so, they will be able to realize the financial and productivity benefits that come with it.

CHAPTER 5

Finding a Contract and Marketing

Independent contracting stems from a base of knowledge. That base will vary according to the nature of the particular contractor segment. Independent contracting can also be a very lucrative industry as well as exciting for its participants. There is a well developed market with firms that are seeking innovative solutions to business and development challenges whether they are in the for-profit, non-profit or government sectors. The demand for individuals with expert knowledge, experience or specialized skills is growing stronger every year.

Working as an independent contractor permits you the unique opportunity to "take ownership of your career." You will be your own boss, be able to work pretty much anywhere and from anywhere that you want to. You will be able to set a flexible work schedule to suit your own lifestyle aspirations. Within reason you will determine your own remuneration and how it is paid. If you manage your finances properly, you will be in a position to accept or decline contracts as you wish putting you clearly in control of your own career.

There are of course challenges to be faced as well. It is important that you continually strive to differentiate your skills and services in order to make the short list of applicants. Competition from other consultants is often very tough and you are not guaranteed a monthly salary, particularly as you begin your business. There are the usual risks of business as clients often do not require your services on a regular basis resulting in periods of down-time for you. As I have also found, despite doing good quality work and perhaps making/saving your client thousands of dollars, they will be slow in paying you and perhaps they will not pay you at all!

Despite the potential hurdles, many independent contractors have found the formula to a successful career and are well sought after. There are also some contractors that continuously struggle to find work and make a go of it. The question then is what makes for a successful independent contractor? The answer lies in how an individual develops and manages their livelihood. Essentially, they must "take ownership of their career" in order to navigate the obstacles that might hold them back from success.

Preparing to be an Independent Contractor

In many cases the difference in working as an employee to that of a contractor will be negligible in terms of the conditions you will be working in. You do need to do a paradigm shift in your thought processes. You will now need to be thinking as a business person rather than thinking as an employee.

The employer/payer organization depends on the contractor to further the products and services that they provide to their market and the internal processes to accomplish that. Their ability to accomplish their goals and objectives is impacted by the quality of the services and advice they receive from the consultants they hire. What is it then that the employer is looking for in hiring you as an independent contractor?

What the Employer/Payer is looking for:

There are three major issues that the employer is looking to accomplish by hiring an independent contractor rather than another employee.

First, the employer/payer looks to the consultant to provide an expertise that is not available currently within the organization. Generally the expertise is only needed periodically and as such the position will not warrant the hiring of a full time employee. This means that you will need to bring specific skills to the task and be prepared to be looking for a new assignment in a short period of time.

Second, the employer/payer may be looking for an independent assessment of programs, projects or processes that the company has undertaken or is considering undertaking. An outside individual may bring a different perspective to the organization and assist in the development of the appropriate practices to develop the guidelines to be followed. You will need to have some analytical skills to identify problems and be able to present a workable solution on a timely basis.

Third, there may be functions or services that may be considered less than economical to conduct internally. This can be considered from both the time and/or the cost perspectives. Your skill set should be such that you are filling a need or a gap in the organizations current capabilities.

How do you meet these needs?

Developing Your Career

In my career, there was a requirement to obtain a university degree that provided a basic core of knowledge. This was supplemented with additional training that led to writing a uniform set of national final exams. On the job training and employer sponsored in-house programs were designed to teach you how to prepare a corporate year end working paper file leading to the annual financial statements and related tax returns.

Once you successfully completed the uniform final exams and you received your designation, there was a monitored requirement to attend annual courses to maintain your technical level of expertise. These courses all related to the technical accounting and tax issues allowing us to provide first rate services to our clients. I heard many of my colleagues say on finally receiving their designation that now they could start to learn what the profession was really all about. None of the professional development courses taught us how to operate an accounting practice. The issues of negotiating leases, buying equipment, maintaining the technology, hiring and in some cases firing employees and all the other related concerns were left to trial and error.

It is similar with an independent contractor business. Entrepreneurship, of which consulting is a subset is not a formal discipline. As such the acquisition of consulting skills and expertise remains pretty much an experiential process. Gaining this experience remains the responsibility of the individual consultant. It will be your responsibility to develop your technical knowledge and skills required to understand your target market and learn how to deploy those skills to the benefit of your clients.

If you have read through chapters 2, 3 and 4 you will have learned that there are benefits to you to operate as an independent contractor. These benefits include a compelling financial advantage as well as numerous other benefits that are less susceptible to quantification. You will have also learned the beauty of the win/win aspect with the benefits to the organization that employs you as an independent contractor.

Despite the benefits, you need to realize that being an independent contractor is not the same as having a regular job. You are a "plug and play personnel" hired to provide expert knowledge and/or certain skills for a specified period of time. The length of the contract can vary based on various economic or technological considerations.

Just as I needed the University education and the designation to become a credible independent contractor, you will not likely succeed without a basis of a solid education background combined with a proven track record of experience and a specialized skill set. Your qualifications serve as an indicator of what you know and how well you know your area of expertise. While a great attitude and perhaps a willingness to work hard over time to gain work experience will help to compensate for low grades, you must remember that you are competing against some of the best in your field. In addition to continually maintaining technical competence, you need to consider the soft skills of analytical and strategic thinking that are vital to your success as an independent contractor.

The first path to becoming an independent contractor is to excel in your academic endeavors. Your accomplishments in schooling will serve as a strong indication of what you know and your knowledge of your chosen subject matter. In many cases a postgraduate (Masters or Doctorate) degree would of great benefit. This is quite common in the business administration and international consulting scenarios.

While imperative to have a good education behind you, several years of relevant work experience is also an absolute requirement. This work experience needs to be in the area that you are providing services. In the early 2000's, I was giving seminars in the advantages of independent contracting at the University of Alberta Faculty of Extension. Several of my clients were in attendance at these seminars. They had taken time off contracting to attend school full time to develop new web-based skills. In speaking with these clients a few months later, most of them found it difficult to find work using their newly learned skills. Despite many years of experience, many of them operating as independent contractors, they were now competing in an area where they had an education but no practical experience. The result is that they were forced to compete with people just graduating from school with no prior experience.

If you are just starting out you might consider the other path being to obtain a position as a practitioner in your chosen field. You need to assess your own skills and competencies. Perhaps you can obtain some professional work experience by obtaining work as a sub-consultant to a more established consultant; who can be used to help launch you into your own practice once you have gained a certain degree of experience and confidence.

Starting employment with a consulting firm will provide you with an opportunity to learn how the work is to be approached. You may be fortunate to find a mentor to guide you. This will allow you to commit yourself to learning the nature of the business and the necessary skills for your field. This gives you the occasion to get involved in consulting work and then to consistently apply and sharpen your skills. Be creative and try to strive to excel with whatever you are given.

Be open to feedback as that is what will make you a good consultant. In my own profession, the quality control function was extremely important; so much so that my office always had a two designated accountant review of all corporate work. While the feedback may have seemed at times like constant criticism, it was how we all learned what was acceptable and it was how we maintained a high level of quality in the work we did for our clients. It was like tough love and you could take it as a negative or use it to further your knowledge and skills.

There is obviously no substitute for knowledge to be successful as a consultant. You however, also need to develop your skills and experience where there are major needs and gaps in the resources (people) with the tools to meet those needs. Armed with this, you will set yourself apart from the competition and be well on the way to success as an independent contractor.

Other considerations in preparing for your career

Money is the lifeblood of any business! Without a regular income business will grind to a halt. Therefore, being successful as an independent contractor is highly dependent on you having a steady stream of work. There will, of course, be times when you have a gap between contracts. Hopefully these periods of downtime will be short lived. There are a number of things that you can do to ensure that you always have work ahead of you.

<u>Personal Presence</u>

You should look the part! If you want to be a professional consultant/contractor then you should dress the part. That means that you should dress as the business executives in the industry you serve would dress. You really don't want to dress the way the ordinary employee is dressed. You want to reflect that you bring more to your client.

You should definitely invest in your business wardrobe. Through your appearance, you want to convey, with clothes and accessories you wear, that you are successful at your contracting practice. Appearance is very important to portray a professional image to your clients. Try to avoid those things that detract from your personal appearance. Stay away from wearing flashy jewelry, gaudy watches and severely tailored suits that are not likely to be accepted in your consulting marketplace. You really want to dress comparably to the executive level of your client and dress like people you respect as peers in the consulting industry.

It is typical to attend a job interview dressed in a business suit. You do this because you want to impress your potential client. Every day when you go to work, you are presenting yourself not only to your client, but to your client's client. Is there any reason why your daily dress should be any different than the day you made your first impression?

Some things that you should perhaps consider along this line include: possibly looking into a weight reduction program or whether you need to update your wardrobe and accessories that go with it. All in all, your personal presence consists of how you dress, how you conduct yourself, how you use your voice, and how other people experience your qualities when you are with them. Generally speaking, people are more comfortable with people that are like them, so you should dress and conduct yourself accordingly.

Niche Market

It has been said that no niche market is too small. To be successful when you're competing against numerous people who have a similar skill set to your skill set, you need to find ways to distinguish yourself from the herd.

My accounting practice was always a general practice, however, it was not until I embraced the independent contractor market that I was able to make any real money. I was able to do so not only because I directed marketing, staffing, and workflow efforts towards the needs of the independent contractor, but because in doing so I was able to establish services designed specifically for the independent contractor. Through providing seminars, writing articles and conducting numerous face-to-face meetings with independent contractors, I was able to develop an in-depth knowledge of the issues that the new consultant faced on start up as well as the unique investment requirements faced by my successful clients as their companies matured.

You should perhaps start by taking an audit of your own skill set. You must know what your own competencies are. Review your resume and list the various positions that you have held through the years. Create a list of the variety of skills that you needed in order to accomplish this work. This analysis will help you to see what you're good at and the skills that you have. Your next step is then to determine what you can do with those skills to benefit a client. You need to study the market and define your own niche where your skills are required.

Make sure that you are offering unique services. If you are a generalist providing the same services that other established independent contractors are already offering, you will be having to fight against other competition. On the other hand, if you develop skills and knowledge in an area where few if any others are specializing, as I did with the independent contractor market, you will find it is much easier to develop alliances with other people who will recommend you and you will feel more confident yourself that you are meeting the needs of your particular clients.

<u>Other Skills</u>

If you have audited your skill set and you have determined that you do have knowledge and skills that you feel confident to offer in a consulting marketplace, your next step is to project into the future to try and determine what additional skills you must learn. It is important to not only consider the current requirements, but also to proactively anticipate what you will need further down the road to allow you to continue to deliver quality services to your clients.

At any given time you will have a certain level of technical competence. You need to ensure that you can maintain this technical competence as well as to keep up with both technological and economic changes. If you find that you have some deficiency in your current or future skill sets, then perhaps you need to enroll in a course or a conference that will ensure your ongoing technical competence.

Of course technical competence is only one of the skill sets that you will require when operating as an independent contractor. Your technical skills need to be complemented by "soft skills" i.e. "people skills" in order to ensure top performance. Individuals who demonstrate great soft skills will always be in high demand. Because as an independent contractor it is essential for you to learn these skills, employers continue to look favorably on hiring independent contractors rather than full-time employees.

You must always keep the needs of your clients foremost in your mind. Independent contracting is about providing solutions to problems. You will find a higher success rate, if you are a competent problem solver. This requires an analytical mind and the ability to ask relevant questions in order to root out the causes of your client's problems. In some cases, your client may not even be aware they have a problem but it becomes your professional responsibility to define the issues for your client.

From a business perspective an independent contractor needs to refine his or her negotiation skills. You need to have a clear understanding of the working arrangements and timelines with respect to your assignment. You will also need to research the going market rate for the services that you are offering. This will make it more practical to arrive at a win–win solution that will accommodate both your concerns and those of your clients.

You will find that basic writing skills are essential as an independent contractor. If you're going to be successful, you need to improve your writing skills. Reports that are poorly written, will be rejected by your client while well written reports are embraced. It does take time to master report writing and you'll find that some clients favor one form over another. The only way to master the art of writing is to write. I have always found it beneficial to have someone else proofread my work before I present it to the ultimate user.

Similar to writing skills, the ability to deliver a comprehensive presentation in an oral manner can become the difference between winning and losing the contract. You don't necessarily have to be a great speaker although the content of your presentation must be powerful, engaging and persuasive. When you speak you need to show a confidence in your subject and maintain eye contact with your audience. It is been said that most people would rather be in the pine box than delivering the eulogy. Almost everyone has the jitters before giving a presentation to more than one individual. I began providing seminars for independent contractors, along with Brenda Douglas of HDF Financial (an insurance company based in Edmonton, Alberta) to show them the benefits of independent contracting and the insurance requirements and employee benefits that go along with it. You really wouldn't want to have been very close to us before our first presentation. We got through that first delivery in good shape and found that our message was well received by everyone in attendance. We soon became very comfortable in making a delivery more because we had a compelling message than any particular speaking ability that we had.

Any time an individual is looking for a job, they go through the process of selling themselves and/or their services to a potential buyer. It is no different as an independent contractor except that perhaps you'll be going through the marketing process more frequently. As with your pitch to be an employee, you need to present a compelling value proposition for your client in order to solve his needs and/or problems. Although I believe they were few and far between with my clients, business cards and perhaps professionally designed flyers or brochures that describe your services are always a good take away for your prospective client. Only a few of my clients establish their own website, however I have found that a supplier's website is one of the first places people review when looking to hire someone. Social media rampant as it is today is also a good way to advertise yourself. You should be particularly cautious as to the information you put out about yourself in these forums, because you never know who will be using them and what impression they will leave.

It is not uncommon for independent contractors to be working side-by-side with employees and other consultants as part of the team. This is particularly true with information technology consultants. It is important to remember to focus on the ultimate goal and play your part and support your other team members. The outcome will be the result of the collective effort. Even if you are assigned the leadership of the team you must remember that your job is first and foremost that of an advisor. It is still your client's project. Leadership skills will become vital to you in these circumstances. Hopefully they will enable you to guide your team towards the successful completion of your assignment. Strong leadership skills, such as the ability to listen, guide and motivate your team to a successful completion of the project are things that you need to develop.

It is essential that you stay on top of your skills by identifying your career development needs. You need to keep your resume current and review it periodically for clues that may guide you in developing your business strategy. Regardless of what field you're in, a successful independent contractor should maintain the highest ethics and professionalism standards available.

★ ★ ★ ★ ★

How Do I Find A Contract as an Independent Contractor?

If you have some specific knowledge or skills, at least three to five years of related work experience and you understand the benefits of contracting as a form of working relationship, then you will want to know what steps to take to take advantage of the benefits.

Your first step is to secure a contract. I suggest that you get something concrete in place before you begin the incorporation process. I had several clients that set up a company and never did follow through with finding a contract.

It is most common that an independent contractor will work for a single client at any point of time. This is generally the most economical format as you will likely be working full days continuously throughout the period of your contract. This work will most likely be for a large company and you'll be working with many other contractors as well as full-time employees.

Some contractors will opt to work for smaller businesses. They will generally find that their contracts will more likely be part time or for shorter periods. Smaller businesses simply cannot afford the rates required by an independent contractor and expect them to work full-time. The contractor who concentrates on the smaller business will have to work harder to market his services and will likely experience less than full-time employment. He is less likely to have open gaps between contracts than a consultant working for a large company; however he may not be working full days or full weeks.

There are many ways to keep your name out there and ways to find contracts. I believe that networking is the way that most contractors find a contract and often it leads to the better contracts. Word–of–mouth through your contacts opens opportunities for you before the position is offered publicly. Placement firms are perhaps the next best source for finding contracts.

Networking

Successful independent contracting depends upon the creation of mutually beneficial business relationships. Networking is without a doubt the number one means for an independent contractor to find a contract. If you are just starting out, you may not have built up a network of people that you can go to in order to learn about who is hiring and who is not. Even before you decide to become an independent contractor, it is very important to start generating a network of people that you feel comfortable going to as and when you're looking for a contract.

Networking, of course, is much more than simply finding people that can help you when you need help. You're probably well aware that your success as a contractor is not, and will not be solely because of your knowledge and skills. Much of your success stems from the relationships that you have with your superiors, peers, and fellow workers within the company or companies that you work for. Networking is much more than just who you know. Your relationship should be a mutually respectful connection that exists between you. It would be prudent for the novice contractor to develop a lot of new relationships fairly quickly.

Networking is a powerful way to grow your consulting business as it increases the number of your relevant business contacts that may lead to consulting assignment leads and referrals. Maintaining relationships with your current industry contacts help you to maintain a positive level of business. Keeping in regular touch with your contacts is essential. You need to be constantly on the lookout for opportunities to expand your network of contacts in order to ensure that your business will continue to grow. You should always be proactively looking for opportunities to open communication lines with your peers and associates and to exchange business cards. Simply being in the same room with your peers is not an adequate step in networking. You must approach them and engage them in discussion of what they do, what you do, and perhaps how your resources can be mutually beneficial. Always keep your relationship professional even if it extends to activities outside the workplace.

Always try to have lunch with someone that may become a referral source. A lot of contractors will work in teams and often that team will go out to lunch together. Even if you're paying only for your own meal, this is a great networking opportunity making the expense of your meal a legitimate deductible expense. Because you went to lunch that day with the team, someone at the table may remember you for a contract down the road or they may be the very person that turns out hiring you. What you want to achieve is to keep your name in front of your contacts so that your name will be the first on their mind if they either have a consulting opportunity, allowing you to work with them or if they can refer you to someone else who has an opportunity for you. The absolute key to networking is that it's not a one-way street. You must be prepared to offer benefits to your contacts before you can expect them to look after you.

If you have a network, you have people to go to that you know and more importantly, they know you. It's a much warmer relationship then making a cold call to a company that has never heard about you. During your networking time, you have the opportunity to make a contact or contacts aware of your capabilities and whatever accomplishments you've achieved. In many cases the business associates may already be well respected individuals in your industry, in which case their word as a referral will carry a fair bit of weight.

Networking has the added benefit that meeting and discussing technical matters with your colleagues provides you not only with up-to-date knowledge of your market, but it will assist in keeping you up to date with the technical knowledge required for the development of your career.

In developing your network, you will want to seek out the people that you have worked with either as a peer or under their tutelage. Keep in mind that when you are looking for a new contract, the people in your network may not be in a position where they can help you or they may not be associated with your target market, at that time. It is then that you have to look to other options to find new work.

<u>Placement Firms</u>

For a beginning contractor, consider using a placement firm to obtain that first contract. I maintained close connections with many of the prominent firms in Edmonton. They were certainly instrumental in helping me develop my practice that specialized in services for the independent contractor. They generally did a very good job for the contractors, particularly those just starting out without any extensive contacts in their industry.

Employers come to placement firms to find employees and contractors. There are some placement firms that specialize strictly in employment positions, and others that only place independent contractors. Other firms will handle both types of positions and can be just as effective as those that specialize in contractors only. The advantage of using a placement firm is that they are well attuned to the marketplace and generally have a substantial list of placements that they are looking to fill. You must still have the appropriate skill set and experience that will make you attractive for the employer. A placement firm generally has the resources to assist you in preparing a resume that will meet the requirements of the position you are applying for. They may also act as an advocate for you if they feel that you meet the criteria for the position. Other placement firms simply act as "order takers" and will provide you with no assistance other than placing your name forward for consideration.

A placement firm obviously receives a commission for placing you with an employer. The amount of their commission generally runs from an absolute low of about 15% to approximately 40% of your hourly rate. Going through a placement firm is therefore somewhat expensive for an employer, as opposed to hiring you directly. On the other hand, it does minimize the time, energy and cost associated with the search for new personnel. Advertising for new employees or contractors can be hit or miss for an organization, depending on how and when they advertise. A placement firm has a ready list of potential personnel to fill most positions and the good firms will do a substantial vetting of the prospects. This is a significant advantage for an employer.

Other marketing steps

While networking and placement firms will generate approximately 95% of the contracts that you will be looking for as an independent contractor, there are other options that you should not overlook. These other options will generally be of more importance if you start to grow your business beyond that of independent contractor to become more of a consulting firm. Nevertheless, you should consider them at all times.

Print media such as newspapers, tender advertisements, and local or regional business magazines are still common means for client organizations to advertise their requirements. You should subscribe to popular newspapers in your city or market area and browse them on a daily basis to ensure that you do not miss any tender advertisements. Local and regional business magazines may also run newsletters or websites that carry advertisements of potential consulting jobs. You should try to get onto the mailing list of any such newsletters.

Electronic media has become a gold mine of information for job seekers. You should regularly visit client websites to monitor when they are looking for potential employees or contractors. Keep in mind that while a position is advertised as being employment, you may be able to make the case to the employer to hire you as an independent contractor. You will find that in addition to client websites there are websites that are dedicated to listing open jobs in various industries. Some of these websites can be accessed free of charge while others may charge a subscription and provide you with options for periodic notification of postings.

Professional and trade organization membership and participation can be an excellent lead source, if you handle it correctly. You want to look for an organization that will have participation by the decision-makers employed in your target market and you want to be proactive in that organization such that you become well know to these decision-makers. You should get involved in committee efforts and be an asset to that Association. Your membership in a professional or trade organization beyond being a rich referral source increases the circle of influence that you have in your target market. You do need to be cautious in that your participation in the activities of the Association can be time-consuming and unless you are working with the right people, your efforts will not be productive in generating work for yourself.

I believe that every independent contractor should have their own website. Today, virtually everyone has access to the web and is most likely to look there first for information with respect to a particular individual or business. It becomes an online resume for you. Your website will provide good general information for potential employers and provide them with a way to contact you. It also has the ability for you to provide "tips" for use by your clients and a means for you to demonstrate your knowledge in a particular area or information about your skills. Again a caution in that a website must be kept up to date. To do so requires the devotion of both time and effort that may become onerous as time moves on. The website may also be an expense that exceeds its benefits, particularly for somebody starting their contracting business.

An online "blog" (newsletter) can be an effective means of presenting your knowledge or expertise to potential clients. If they have seen and read your blogs before you make an application for a position, it will be as if they already know you. That places you one level above the cold call. Unfortunately, in today's world, we are inundated with so much reading material that unless your blogs are interesting and compelling for the intended readers it may never be viewed.

The consultant whose business has grown beyond that of the independent contractor may find that advertising services in print or electronic media is a viable option. It will be necessary to prepare and post a compelling profile of your services and your expertise. This may require the services of a professional media writer or advertising firm. The cost and the potential return on this sort of advertising would be nominal for somebody operating as an independent contractor. I am not aware that any of my clients tried this option, so I am unable to speak to the ultimate success of this marketing strategy.

The more established independent contractor will tend to get work through referrals and repeat business. In many cases, what starts out as a short term contract will often get extended or renewed because the employer is satisfied with the work that you've done on their behalf. Referrals and repeat business are perhaps the surest way to build your business and your professional reputation. You should always strive to do a good job and satisfy your clients which will allow you to gain their confidence and loyalty.

★ ★ ★ ★ ★

CHAPTER 6

Forms of Organization

Congratulations, you have decided to make the leap of faith and become an independent contractor. You have decided to "take ownership of your career!"

Traditionally, when I started specializing with independent contractors the referrals would come from a placement firm. During meetings with the key recruiters at several of the leading placement firms in town, I had put across the proposition that we had a unique program for independent contractors which started with assisting them with starting up their own corporation. This seemed to give the recruiter a reason to send a new contractor to me (to get incorporated) and in turn gave me the opportunity to inform the client about our distinctive program.

As the client had been sent to me for the express purpose of becoming incorporated, I was always concerned whether or not they had been pushed to this decision or whether they had come to it themselves and were comfortable with it. While incorporation is the correct form of organization in most cases, there are times when it is not the ideal basis of operation for a particular contractor.

Three Forms of Organization

A business entity is an organization that is formed in accordance with the law in order to engage in business activities, usually for the sale of a product or the provision of a service.

There are many types of business entities defined in the legal systems of various countries. These include corporations, cooperatives, partnerships, sole traders, limited liability company, joint ventures and other specialized types of organization. It should be remembered, however, that the regulations governing particular types of entity, even those described as roughly equivalent, may differ to a greater or lesser extent between countries. When creating a business, the type of business entity you choose will undoubtedly influence the legal structure.

There are a number of forms of organization that are available to an independent contractor. In Canada, there are several types of corporation and several forms of partnerships, however there are really only three basic forms of organization that you will want to operate in. These forms are:

1. Proprietorship
2. Partnership, and
3. Incorporation

These forms are very common, but some of you may not be familiar with the terms and many of you will need a clearer outline of what the forms really consist of. A good starting point would therefore be to try to define what each of these types of formation is.

Proprietorship:

A proprietorship, or sole proprietorship as it is more commonly referred to, is the most simple form of business ownership. A proprietor is a person who owns a proprietorship, which is simply a self-employed business. Unlike a corporation, partnership or limited liability corporation, there is no distinction between the individual and his/her business.

A business owned by a single person that is not a corporation, a limited liability company, or anything else. The sole proprietor who owns the proprietorship must list all profits and losses on his/her personal tax return and does not file a separate return for the business. Additionally, the proprietor is personally responsible for all losses and debts the business incurs. Some small businesses often begin as sole proprietorships and then become something else. In many cases, proprietorships are part-time businesses that their owners operate on the side while holding down a full or part-time employment position.

Partnership:

The partnership is the simplest and least expensive co-owned business structure to create and maintain. If you plan to run your small business with a partner, you are not a proprietorship and are instead a partnership. You may create the partnership via a general partnership agreement, but you may not function as a sole proprietorship

Statutory regulation of partnerships in Canada falls under provincial jurisdiction. A partnership is not a separate legal entity and partnership income is taxed at the rate of the partner receiving the income. It can be deemed to exist regardless of the intention of the partners. Common elements considered by courts in determining the existence of a partnership are that two or more legal persons are carrying on a business in common with a view to a profit.

By definition, a partnership is a business with more than one owner that has not filed papers with the federal or provincial jurisdiction to become a corporation. There are two basic types of partnerships: general partnerships and limited partnerships. With respect to independent contractors we are only concerned with general partnerships; the more familiar structure in which every partner has a hand in managing the business.

Corporations (Incorporated companies):

I vividly recall in one of my early accounting courses at university (Strange what sticks with you!), one of my classmates was asked to define what a corporation is. His simple answer that it is "a legal fiction" left us all in stitches. The answer however is surprisingly correct. This is primarily a reflection that the "corporation" has a life of its own, separate and apart from the owners of that organization.

The Corporation is the most common form of business organization in Canada. It is defined as an organization which is chartered by the federal or a provincial jurisdiction and given many legal rights as an entity separate from its owners. This form of business is characterized by the limited liability of its owners, the issuance of shares of easily transferable stock, and existence as a going concern. The process of becoming a corporation (called incorporation) gives the company separate legal standing from its owners and protects those owners from being personally liable in the event that the company is sued (a condition known as limited liability). Incorporation also provides companies with a more flexible way to manage their ownership structure. In addition, there are different tax implications for corporations. Some of these tax issues can be beneficial while others may be detrimental. In these respects, corporations differ from sole proprietorships and limited partnerships.

A **corporation** is an organization formed with governmental approval to act as an artificial person to carry on business (or other activities), which can sue or be sued, and can issue shares of stock to raise funds with which to start a business or increase its capital. Ownership of a corporation is determined by the holding of share capital (capital stock) in a corporation. The company is incorporated with articles that specify the amount and type(s) of capital stock that may be issued. Each type of stock is assigned rights and privileges that determine the stock holders' ability to influence the operations of the company. Many people that incorporate their own company for operation as an independent contractor will set up an inappropriate share structure and most fail to actually issue share capital. Unless and until shares are issued, no one owns the company. An inappropriate share structure may prevent you from properly allocating income in a tax efficient manner. These are issues that need to be rectified immediately.

★ ★ ★ ★ ★

Characteristics of the Forms of Organization

To better understand the three forms of organization it would be beneficial to review and compare some of their major characteristics as follows:

Formation and Cost to Set Up:

<u>Proprietorship</u>

A proprietorship has a very low cost to set up. You basically start running your business and contact Revenue Canada to set up your payroll and HST/GST accounts, if applicable.

Although you can operate your business under your own name, a proprietorship is typically not run under the name of the owner. Instead, the business typically uses a "trade name." The trade name should be searched through the provincial registry office to ensure that it does not conflict with another business already in existence. An example of this would be if John Smith owned a photography business called "Johnny's Photos." The Name "Johnny's Photos" should be searched through the registry office and registered as a trade name. For his bank to accept cheques made out to "Johnny's Photos," John would likely need to file paperwork with the registry office so that the trade name can be traced back to John and his Social Insurance Number. With the trade name filed, John could open a chequing account in the business' name and advertise the business name knowing that he owns the rights to it.

Depending on your location, you may also require a business license to operate a business in your municipality.

<u>Partnership:</u>

A partnership is also generally low cost to start up. You do need to contact Revenue Canada for your tax accounts and you should also consider the registration of the partnership through the provincial registry office to facilitate banking and other arrangements.

You don't have to file any paperwork to establish an ordinary partnership -- just agreeing to go into business with another person will get you started.

Of course, partnerships must meet the same local registration requirements as any new business. Most cities and counties require businesses to register with them and pay at least a minimum business tax.

In addition, as with a proprietorship, your partnership may have to register a fictitious or assumed business name. If your business name doesn't contain all of the partners' last names (for instance, you want to use "Canada Landscape Photography" instead of "Smith & Jones Landscape Photos"), you usually must register that trade name also known as a fictitious or assumed business name with the provincial registry office.

While the owners of a partnership are not legally required to have a written partnership agreement, it makes good sense to put the details of ownership, including the partners' rights and responsibilities and their share of profits, into a written agreement. If you don't have a written agreement in place, provincial legislation may dictate the rights, privileges and profit shares. This agreement may increase your cost to set up as you will incur legal fees to create or at least vet your agreement.

One disadvantage of partnerships is that when one partner wants to leave the company, the partnership generally dissolves. In that case, the partners must fulfill any remaining business obligations, pay off all debts, and divide any assets and profits among themselves.

In order to avoid this what might be an untimely ending for your business, you should create a buy-sell agreement, or buyout agreement, which can be included as part of your partnership agreement. A buy-sell/buyout agreement helps partners decide and plan for what will happen when one partner retires, dies, becomes disabled, or leaves the partnership to pursue other interests. For example, such an agreement might allow the partners to buy out a departing partner's interest, so business can continue as usual. This will of course, add to the overall cost of starting up the business.

A partnership may be formed by individuals. It is also possible that one or more of the partners may be a limited liability corporation rather than an individual.

Corporation:

The corporation is generally a little more expensive to start than either a partnership or a proprietorship depending on how you go about it. In most provinces, you are able to do your own registration of your company. The company will require a distinct name and as such a name search must be done through the registry office and then registered when the "articles of incorporation" are filed. The "articles of incorporation" set out the share structure, the rights and privileges of each of the classes of authorized share capital and may also set out rules for the disposal of shares and other issues such as the maximum number of directors and shareholders that the company may have. Unless you are very knowledgeable about how to do this, I strongly recommend against doing the incorporation yourself. In fact, I got started doing client incorporations because when I started working with independent contractors, I sent each of the first three clients to lawyers for the incorporation. In each case, they came back with a corporate structure that was not appropriate for the type of company that was needed. If lawyers can't get it right, how do you suppose that you will? Generally when a client incorporated their own company, they failed to issue capital stock (so no one really owned their company and they had no right to dividends) and had no documentation to appoint officers and directors of the company. These are very basic documents that need to be prepared.

Depending on whether you opt for a federal corporation or a provincial company, you can start your own company for about $500 give or take. A lawyer will charge upwards of $1,000 for the incorporation, but that will include a complete minute book detailing the initial director and shareholder meetings.

After the third client came back from his lawyer and I indicated the shortcomings of the share structure, his lawyer called me and asked what he needed to do to fix the problem. I advised him as to what needed to be done and what the share structure should look like. He charged my client $1,350 for that incorporation and I got nothing but the following fourteen years of corporate work for that client. That fee was in 1997, so the cost will have increased substantially since then. It was at this point that I started to do the incorporation for my clients. My fee started around $500 and ended up at approximately $750; almost enough to cover my time and out of pocket registration costs. This included a full minute book including share certificates.

Accountants will generally charge a midrange fee if they do incorporations at all. Incorporation at one time was considered to be the purview of a lawyer and was considered legal work. Professional accountants were reluctant to be holding themselves out as doing legal work. As the registration has become privatized, it is readily apparent that incorporation is now the administrative responsibility of the corporate secretary and the function can be outsourced to accountants who are often in a better position to do incorporation than a lawyer. I suggest that you look for an accountant that has extensive experience working with independent contractors otherwise they may make the same mistakes that the lawyers my clients used did.

The business operated by your company represents your personal efforts and ultimately your personal income. As such, I never recommend that anyone besides a spouse be a shareholder of your independent contractor company. Even then you need to consider the stability of the relationship. I have been advised by a lawyer that your company is considered "community property" and as such even if the spouse has no share ownership, they would be entitled to 50% of the value of the company on marriage dissolution.

Some consultants want to have their child as a shareholder. I also discourage this option. If the child is under eighteen years of age, any distribution to him/her will be caught by the Canadian "kiddy tax."

Under this provision, the distribution is taxed in the child's hands at the top personal tax rates. It may make some sense if your child is over eighteen and attending post-secondary education. You will be able to split some income to them to be taxed at their minimal personal tax rate rather than at your higher tax rate. Unfortunately, once they graduate, they will (hopefully) have their own income and it is no longer an advantage to siphon off income to them. It is a little more difficult to remove a shareholder. To redeem their shares, you would need to pay them the "fair market value" of their shares which could be a substantial amount. On dissolution of the company, your child would likely be entitled to a certain portion of the company assets depending on the rights assigned to their shares in the Articles of Incorporation.

Separate Legal Entity?

Proprietorship and Partnership:

The proprietorship and the partnership do not have a separate existence from their principal(s). They are in fact an extension of the principal(s). A proprietorship will cease to exist on the demise of its owner.

A partnership may have a specified termination date as per the written partnership agreement or on the retirement or withdrawal of one or more partners. The agreement may be able to extend the existence of the organization as partners are admitted or retired from the partnership. This is often the case in larger partnerships such as some large accounting firms or law firms.

Corporation:

A corporation as my classmate had indicated; is a legal fiction. The corporation continues to exist beyond the demise of one or more of its owners. It is recognized as a separate legal entity that is separate and apart from its owner(s).

Sheltered Liability?

Proprietorship:

One of the biggest dangers of running a business as a proprietorship is that the owner is fully responsible for all of the legal and financial liabilities of the business. If an employee gets hurt on the job and sues the business, they will sue the owner personally, not the business. If a business loan is acquired or commercial debts are incurred and the business fails, the proprietor will still be on the hook for repaying the debt.

Partnerships:

All of the partners are personally liable for all business debts and obligations, including court judgments of the business. This means that if the business itself can't pay a creditor, such as a supplier, lender, or landlord, the creditor can legally come after any partner's house, car, or other possessions of the owners.

There are a few exceptions to this personal liability. In certain partnerships, there are people who are simply investors and do not take part in the operations. This situation is generally related to large operations such as real estate or oil and gas projects. In these cases, some of the partners can have limited personal liability if the partnership is set up as a limited partnership. This is a partnership in which only the general partner, who runs the business, has personal liability, while the limited partners, who are basically passive investors, can lose no more than their stake in the partnership. This type of partnership is not generally applicable for an independent contractor/consulting style of business. Businesspeople who are particularly concerned about personal liability normally choose to incorporate their business.

Another major concern is that any individual partner can usually bind the whole business to a contract or other business deal. For instance, if your partner signs a year-long contract with a supplier to buy inventory at a price your business can't afford, you can be held personally responsible for the money owed under the contract.

The partnership agreement may attach limits to a partners ability to bind the partnership, however, unless an outsider has reason to know of any limits the partners have placed on each other's authority in their partnership agreement, any partner can bind the others to a deal.

It should be noted that one of the restrictions on this ability to bind the partnership relates to the sale of the partnerships assets. One partner cannot bind the partnership to a sale of all of the partnership's assets.

Finally joint liability is also a concern. Each individual partner can be sued for and be required to pay the full amount of any business debt. This is known as "joint and several liability." A creditor may go after a partner with the deepest pockets. If this happens, an individual partner's only recourse may be to sue the other partner or partners for their shares of the debt.

This combination of personal liability for all partnership debt and the authority of each partner to bind the partnership make it vital that you trust the people with whom you start your business. People can change when things start to go bad.

Corporation:

A corporation offers the most protection when it comes to commercial liability. A corporation's liability for damages or debts is limited to its assets, so the shareholders and officers are protected from personal claims, unless they commit fraud.

When the protection from liability is permitted we are generally considering a company with multiple shareholders. In most cases some or all of the owners (shareholders) may not have any say in or be aware of the day to day operations of the company. Except through reports provided by those who have been charged with the management of the company as a director and/or an officer of the company, these shareholders have no knowledge as to what the company is doing. Under these circumstances, it seems only right that the shareholder should be protected from liability for the debts of the company through its operations.

For the independent contractor/consultant, you need to take the corporate liability shelter with a grain of salt. Generally an independent contractor/consultant will incorporate with himself/herself as the sole director and sole shareholder or alternatively with the spouse as a shareholder and or director. The company is incorporated in this manner to permit the ability to split income between the two spouses. It is rare that a third party or even another member of the family is a shareholder or director of the company. In these circumstances, the contractor/consultant is not entirely dealing at "arm's length" (independent of the company) with the company. Because of this conflict, they will have more liability than otherwise anticipated.

A company director, whether in a small corporation or a large corporation, can be held personally liable for the payment of source deductions and HST/GST that the company fails to pay. These amounts are considered trust funds collected on behalf of the federal government. It is the responsibility of the corporate directors to ensure that these amounts are remitted to the government on a timely basis.

In a small closely held company, if the company requires funds that necessitate borrowing from a financial institution, it is almost a foregone conclusion that the lender will require personal guarantees. They may require these guarantees not only from the shareholder/director, but also from a spouse whether or not they are connected with the company. At one point, when I was looking for a new operating line of credit with the bank, they wanted seven times coverage of the maximum line including a personal guarantee by my wife. At the time my wife was not even working in the practice. She only functioned as the bookkeeper/treasurer for my professional corporation.

The corporation for an independent contractor will incur expenses that may, on average, amount to about 25% of the gross revenue. These expenses do also offset items (house, telephone, automobile, phone and other expenses) that might otherwise be payable personally by the contractor if they were not operating a business. With taxes, there should still be about 60% of gross revenue available to meet investment and personal financial needs of the principal(s). The major withdrawal from the company is for the personal needs of the shareholder(s)/director(s). Prudent management of the company's funds should dictate that enough funds are set aside for contingencies such as a gap between contracts. It is the responsibility of the directors to ensure that the company can meet all of its commercial liabilities. If funds are drawn for personal purposes putting the company in a position where it cannot meet its obligations, then the directors become personally liable for the corporate debts.

On the dissolution of a company, the shareholders take on the liability for any unsatisfied debts if they have drawn funds to jeopardize the ability of the company to meet those obligations.

As such, the contractor needs to pay attention to the debts incurred in the name of the company. Those debts are to be paid before any funds are drawn for personal use.

It is quite typical with independent contractors that you will generate a lot of cash in a short period of time. Your accountant will likely be after you to invest that cash in securities owned by your company rather than withdrawing the funds and paying the high personal tax rates on the personal income generated by the withdrawal. The investments are at risk should your company be sued for any debts or should you be held responsible for any professional failings. As the investments represent a significant asset of the contractor, it would be wise to mitigate the potential for loss through carrying professional liability insurance and/or creating a holding company to hold the investments.

Separate Tax Returns?

<u>Proprietorship and partnerships:</u>

A proprietorship or partnerships are not separate legal entities. The liability for taxes rests with the owners of the business.

Proprietors pay all of their taxes at the personal level, and there are no business income taxes. All business expenses may be written off against the business income per the Income Tax Act and its Regulations, and all of the remaining net profit (the money the proprietor earned as personal income plus any profits left in the business) is considered taxable income for the owner.

Proprietors report their income and business expenses on a set of schedules attached to their annual (T1) personal tax return. There may also be other taxes, such as the contribution to the Canada Pension Plan that are also calculated on the net business income and paid through the personal tax system.

A partnership is not a separate tax entity from its owners either; instead, it's what is called a "pass-through entity." This means the partnership itself does not pay any income taxes on its profits. Business income simply "passes through" the business to the partners, who report their share of the net income (or losses) on their individual income tax returns. The partnership (as with proprietorships as well) may pay other taxes such as payroll source deductions, HST/GST and municipal business taxes through the business. If these taxes are not paid by the business they become the personal liability of the owner(s).

In addition, each partner must make quarterly estimated tax instalments to Revenue Canada based on the prior year's net income each year. If a partnership is large enough, it may also have to file an annual partnership information return.

Corporations:

Corporations are a separate legal entity from their owners. As such, there is one or more annual corporate tax returns to be filed. In Alberta and Quebec a separate provincial corporate tax return must be filed in addition to the federal (T2) income tax return.

As with the proprietorship and the partnership, there may be other taxes to be paid. These are all paid by the corporation. As noted previously, a director can be held personally liable for the payment of source deductions and HST/GST taxes if the company fails to make the appropriate remittances. It is imperative that the shareholder/director of an independent contractor company makes sure these taxes are paid and paid on a timely basis to avoid penalties.

Financial Statements Required?

Proprietorship and partnerships:

Most proprietorships do not require the preparation of annual financial statements. Generally a schedule of income and expenses is prepared for inclusion in the owner's personal tax return. A balance sheet detailing the assets and the liabilities of the business is seldom prepared.

The lack of a balance sheet seems logical in that because it is not a separate legal entity; the assets of the business are the property of the owner. Similarly, the liabilities are also those of the owner. It is often prudent to track these assets and liabilities related to the business, despite the fact that they are not technically owned by the business.

Accounting is often referred to as the language of business. The end result of accounting is the production of a full set of financial statements. The financial statements present the owner with a snapshot to the past experience of the company operations and its current financial position. It is through the objective review of the annual financial statements that the business owner can see the tangible results of past operating activities and it is through this look back that plans can be formulated for what is both necessary and what is feasible going forward. For this reason, I would urge any business owner to prepare a full annual financial statement rather than being content with the tax return schedule. That schedule is often prepared as a statement of receipts and disbursements without reflecting the related accrued income and liabilities.

Should the business owner require financing for either the business or for personal purposes, it is likely that an astute lender will require financial statements beyond the tax return schedules.

As with the proprietorship, there is no requirement to prepare financial statements for a partnership, however for the same reasons it would be wise to prepare an annual set of financial statements. With a partnership it may be even more imperative to have the statements prepared. It is possible that one or more of the partners does not have daily access to the status of the accounting records. The annual statements (whether audited or not) will provide at least an overall view of how the business is doing. It will be more important to track the assets and liabilities as particular partners may have invested more or less towards the assets used by the company than other partners.

The combined efforts of two or more people would reflect a larger operation than a proprietorship business. It is more likely that a partnership will require outside financing for bigger projects. For example; many contractors will go together to allow them to bid on a large contract that perhaps requires different skill sets. In this case it is likely that subcontractors will be hired to provide some of the missing skills. In this case, the partnership may require an operating line of credit to finance the payment for the subcontractors pending invoicing and receipt of payment from the client.

If one or more of the partners is a corporation, that partner will require a set of financial statements to accompany its annual corporate income tax return to support the reported share of income or loss reported for the fiscal year.

<u>Corporations:</u>

Corporations are required under their incorporating legislation to prepare annual "audited" financial statements. Generally the requirement for the statements to be audited can be avoided if the shareholders pass an annual resolution dispensing with the appointment of an auditor and in its place appointing an accountant to prepare the statements on a "Notice to Reader" or "Review" basis.

The corporation is also required to prepare a schedule to its tax return which outlines the details of the financial statements. Any "notes" that accompany the financial statements must be filed with the federal corporate income tax return.

Expense Deductibility

All three forms of organization are permitted to deduct the "amounts laid out to earn income" subject to certain specific restrictions as detailed throughout the Income Tax Act and Regulations as amended from time to time.

It should be noted that it is often easier to support the deduction for a corporation than it might be for a partnership or a proprietorship. For example; to deduct the proportionate share of operating costs for your home (office rent equivalent) Revenue Canada requires that you spend greater than 50% of your time in your home office or that you regularly meet with your clients in that office. This requirement is somewhat arbitrary, completely ignores the reality of the way a business is operated and is certainly not typical with how most independent contractors/consultants function. That being said, it is possible that an inexperienced auditor might disallow your office in the home deduction because you don't meet the above criteria.

Despite the comments above, I was able to successfully argue on behalf of a sole proprietor that used his home office on a very casual basis. He did his own accounting and record keeping as well as some online research while he was at home. During the week he was working on location in Fort McMurray and was not able to be present in his home office in Edmonton most of the time.

Corporations that are properly incorporated will place the records and registered office as that of the home address of the primary shareholder/director. In so doing, you are establishing that this address is where the corporation "lives." It is then not only logical but a necessity that the corporation would be required to pay its share of the office in the home operating expenses. The company under these circumstances should not have to meet the other requirements as set out above.

The issue can become more complicated because if the office in the home deduction is not allowed, then the travel from your home to the client's location may also be disallowed as a deductible expense. Again, as it is a virtual certainty that the corporation should be allowed the deduction, it may be more beneficial to be claiming expenses in a corporation than in a proprietorship or partnership.

Selection of the Fiscal year End and Tax Deferral

Proprietorship and partnerships:

Both a proprietorship and a partnership are required to have a December 31st fiscal year end for tax purposes. As previously noted, these organizations are reported in the personal tax returns of their owner(s). As such, they are required to have a fiscal year end that coincides with the calendar year reporting of the personal income tax return.

Income earned in the current calendar year is required to be reported to December 31st. The net income is taxed in the same calendar year in which it is earned. It cannot be deferred to a sub-sequent fiscal year. While personal income is generally reported on a cash basis, business income is to be reported on the accrual basis. This means that if you have earned income to the end of December, but it is not invoiced or collected until the following year, it is still reported and taxed in the current fiscal year.

Corporations:

The corporation can select any day of the year as its fiscal year end. Normally, the end of a month will be the most convenient as it will then agree to your bank statement and investment statement cut-offs. Since there is really no business cycle for an independent contractor, any month of the year will work for you. As an account-ing practitioner, I did tend to discourage a December fiscal year end. Generally accountants are consumed with T4 and T5 returns in January and February while March and April are busy with per-sonal tax return preparation. As well your accountant will likely be handling an inordinate number of natural December fiscal year ends. This is the period in which you will require the attention of your accountant. Even a January or November fiscal year end will provide your accountant with a better window to look after your needs. This also maximized the time before they would be paying accounting fees for their first fiscal year end.

When I first began working with and incorporating independent contractors, I would indicate that we were not overly busy in the fall. After I quickly went from four to forty September year ends, I changed my approach. If I incorporated a client in August, I would suggest they use July 31st as their fiscal year end. This would extend their yearend out as far as they could allowing for them to earn income August through December of the year of incorporation but deferring the taxation of that income until the following calendar year. The tax on that fiscal year end would not be due until three months after the fiscal year end (October 31st) which provided the contractor with almost fifteen months of tax deferral.

Do I Pay Canada Pension Contributions and Employment Insurance Premiums?

Generally speaking all three forms of organization will result in the payment of Canada Pension Plan contributions. All three forms will withhold the employee portion and remit that together with the employer portion of both Canada Pension (CPP) and Employment Insurance (EI) for any employees that the business may have hired.

For the proprietorship and the partnership, the amount will be calculated in the preparation of the owner's personal tax return and is based on the net income for the fiscal year of the business. The owner will be responsible for both the employee and the employer's portion (matching) of the contributions. The employer portion is allowed as a tax deduction to compensate the individual for paying twice the personal amount.

<u>Proprietorship:</u>

A proprietorship that is contracting through a placement firm is a special situation. It is referred to as "placement agency self-employed" (PASE). What that means is that the individual, contracting through a placement firm, is considered to be self-employed for income tax purposes, but is considered to be an employee for purposes of Canada Pension and Employment Insurance. In this situation, the placement firm is required to withhold both Canada Pension and Employment Insurance from the contractor and remit that together with the employer portion to Canada Revenue Agency.

The amounts withheld and remitted are reported on a T4 Return at the end of each year. The form is marked "PASE" and has a code "11" for the type of payment.

This is not a well known situation even among well experienced accountants. When I started working with placement agencies and independent contractors, one of the agencies began to refer all their contractors to me as I was the only accountant that seemed to understand the issue. There had been several placement agencies that were caught flat-footed in the late 1990s. They had been assessed penalty and interest for failure to remit the amounts that should have been withheld. At a penalty of 10% for the first offense and rising to 20% for second and all subsequent failures, the liability ran quite high for some of these firms.

You should note that the placement firm will charge the contractor for the cost of the remittances. In most cases, it is handled by a slight difference in your hourly rate to compensate for the costs. In some cases however, the placement firm will charge a service fee that strangely equals the amounts they have remitted on your behalf.

Corporations:

Although a corporation will have to pay both CPP and EI for any non-arm's length employees, the owners holding more than 40% of the outstanding shares of the company or those who are related to such a shareholder are not allowed to contribute to Employment Insurance except for the "special benefits" such as maternity, parental, sickness and compassionate care. Some people see this as a liability while some see it as a benefit. In most cases, while a contractor may be between contracts for an extended period of time, most are able to find a new contract before they would become eligible for benefits and would likely have to repay some or all of any such benefits if they did receive compensation.

A shareholder/director does not develop his Canada Pension liability based on the company's net income. It is based on the level of "salary" that they are paid during the year. Many corporate owners will receive their annual remuneration as a dividend payment rather than a salary or in combination with a salary. A dividend is not subject to either CPP or EI withholding or liability. When a salary is however, paid to a shareholder, the company must withhold the employee portion of the Canada Pension contributions and then match it and remit it to Canada Revenue Agency on a timely basis.

Payment of Dividends

Dividends are a return on the investment made in a corporation. There is no corresponding means of remuneration available to a proprietor or a partner.

With a closely held company, the owner(s) have a great deal of flexibility to determine the form that their "annual remuneration" will take. In most provinces in Canada, it is more tax efficient to receive remuneration in the form of a dividend rather than as a salary. As such, most contractors will use a dividend as their form of remuneration or in combination with some amount of salary depending on whether or not they want to contribute to CPP and be eligible to make contributions to a "Registered Retirement Savings Plan." This concept is dealt with in more detail in Chapter 10 – "How Do I Pay Myself?"

★ ★ ★ ★ ★

What Form of Organization Should I Choose?

The best form of organization for you depends on your own circumstances. Generally speaking, you will want to incorporate, however there are circumstances when it might not be your best option.

Why Incorporate:

Incorporation, particularly in the Information Technology sector is how the industry basically works. If you are not incorporated, you are likely cutting out about 90% of your potential market.

Placement firms and most of their larger clients want to work with a corporation rather than an individual. They are particularly sensitive to the issue of having to withhold source deductions and to remit them on a timely basis to avoid costly penalties and interest. We discussed the problem of making those deductions for Canada Pension Plan contributions and Employment Insurance premiums for non-incorporated contractors working through a placement firm in our discussion above.

Most placement firms will allow you the option to incorporate or become a "term employee." A term employee means that you are hired for a specific period of time. You receive no employee benefits aside from CPP and EI. You are not entitled in most cases to any statutory or annual vacation. At the end of your term, you are not entitled to any severance pay if the firm does not retain your services for an extended period. This is not an attractive option. Keep in mind that you don't have to contract through a placement firm. You can subcontract to another contractor or you can contract directly with the client.

There is an additional related concern for placement firms as well. A Canada Revenue Agency audit may result in an assessment of your business as that of a "personal services business" (see Chapter 8). Under such an assessment a sole proprietor will then be considered to be an employee of the placement firm rather than an independent contractor. After the fact, the placement firm will have been required to withhold and remit the CPP, EI and also income tax. If they had been properly withholding and remitting the CPP and EI, they will be onside with those amounts. They will not have withheld and remitted the income tax on your behalf. This could potentially put the placement firm in a position where interest and penalties are also assessed for failure to remit. The placement firm may have their exposure mitigated if you have been paying your personal tax installments on a timely basis, however the placement firm would rather avoid the situation altogether by having you incorporate.

Incorporation also goes a long way to settling the question as to whether or not you are operating as a business (independent contractor) versus an employee. While it is not uncommon for Canada Revenue Agency to assess a corporation as a "personal service business" (PSB) it is not as easy for them to make their case with a corporation as it is with a sole proprietor. This is particularly true if your spouse is also a shareholder and director of your company. It may be possible for a client to control the work of an individual, but if you have another person involved in the ownership/operation of your corporation (but not with the contract under review), it would be virtually impossible for the client to exercise control over that other owner. As you will see in Chapter 8, this would be a criterion that Canada Revenue Agency would have to apply for a PSB assessment to be effective. In the interest of full disclosure, Canada Revenue Agency has ignored this fact and some of at least the lower tax court judges have been close minded about it as well.

Perhaps the greatest reason for incorporation is that there are tax advantages to being incorporated. In Canada we have very low corporate tax rates. The federal rate is about 15% (11% for small businesses). Your company would most likely qualify as a small business corporation eligible for the lower rate. Provincial tax rates vary by province, but the combined rate is generally well below 20%. By comparison the typical tax rate in the United States for a similar company would be about 35%.

Canadian personal tax rates on the other hand are generally relatively high as compared to the country to the South. The corporate rates for funds not currently required and the ability to pay dividends instead or in combination with a salary results in most independent contractors having a combined corporate and personal tax rate of about 14% to 18% of gross revenue.

Why Not Incorporate:

Incorporation is more expensive and requires more record keeping than a proprietorship. Annual accounting fees alone can be close to five times as much for a company as for preparing the personal tax return for a proprietorship. This is a result of the legal requirement for a corporation to have full financial statements prepared annually.

If your hourly rate is not high enough to leave you with a net income that is higher than the top of the low tax bracket for your province, you may miss out on the major tax advantage of the corporation. You have to more closely weigh the advantage and determine if it warrants the extra record keeping.

If the result is not positive for you, then I would suggest postponing incorporation until at least your next contract. You should consider whether or not you intend to continue to operate as an independent contractor.

If that is your career path, it might be worth going ahead with the incorporation. Generally the first contract is the most difficult to obtain, the subsequent contracts come easier as potential clients start to view you as a contractor rather than an employee. If on the other hand, you are just trying out contracting, sometimes because it was offered to you instead of employment, but you are not certain if you will continue when your contract ends, you might consider a proprietorship. Once a corporation is started it is a little bit complicated to dissolve it.

CHAPTER 7

Claiming Expenses as an Independent Contractor

Nature of Independent Contractor Expenses

Aside from accounting fees, virtually all expenses claimed by an independent contractor are the same expenditures that you would be incurring as a full time employee. These expenses include your travel from home to the office or work site and back each day, a portion of your home expenses for a home office, your home computer and all the supplies that go with it, your internet and cell phone and a number of meals and entertainment expenditures. Each of these items is considered a personal expense as an employee, but is a business expense for an independent contractor.

I have always promoted an aggressive treatment for claiming expenses. By this statement I mean that you need to develop the habit of obtaining a receipt to support each expenditure that you make; whether or not you think this expense is for business or personal purposes. Once you have the receipt, you have met the first level of tax audit in that you have support for the expenditure. At this point, you critically examine the nature of the expenditure to determine if it is a business expense or is personal. You have to ask yourself, "How is this expenditure related to my business?" If it has the potential to earn you additional income today or at some point in the future, or to save you an expense today or at some point in the future, it is likely a business expense. It is important to make that paradigm shift in your thinking from that of an employee to that of a business person.

Sometimes expenditures may have both a personal and a business aspect to them. Just because there is a personal side to the expense doesn't mean that you should not be making a claim. In these cases, you should make a reasonable assessment of the portion that would be considered for business and claim that percentage of the total amount. Record only the business portion of the expense.

At no time would I tell you or my clients to deduct something that I don't believe is a business expense. That however, does not mean that Canada Revenue Agency will always agree with me. The government has an army of people telling you what you cannot deduct and they won't tell you that you forgot to deduct some item you have overlooked. They intimidate the taxpayer into being afraid of making a claim for expenses which they are rightfully entitled to claim. If you don't deduct a legitimate expense, you simply lose it and pay too much tax. I generally advise you or my clients to record everything they feel is related to their business when recording their expenses as they otherwise could be missing out on deductions. If you are not claiming everything you are entitled to, then you are overpaying your taxes. Unfortunately, Canada Revenue Agency will only disallow expenses they deem to be not deductible. They will not tell you that you are missing some deductions. Your accountant may question some of the amounts that you have claimed; however, he can't consider items that are not there. Make sure you give him full information about what you are spending for your business.

THE STANDARD CHART OF ACCOUNTS

In my office, we generally used a standard eight step approach to handling the fiscal year end of our clients. In doing so, we gained the efficiency to keep the accounting fees low, giving us a competitive advantage to other accounting firms. At the same time, we were able to maintain a relative high quality in the financial statements and tax returns that we prepared. Inherent in this standard approach is that we asked our clients to follow our standard "chart of accounts." The standard chart of accounts includes accounts for assets, liabilities, equity, revenues and expenses. (See the Contractor's Toolbox - Chapter 13 for the full Chart of Accounts.) The following chart of accounts covers the expenses only and will help you maximize your expense claim and minimize the associated accounting fees. Please note that you may not need all the following accounts or that you need accounts in addition to the following. If you need extra accounts, they can be added, but do not replace one of the following with a new account. Fit the new account in where appropriate.

I have used specific numbering for the accounts. The numbering is not as important as the account description. Numbering helps in locating certain expenses categories. Some accounting software will require the use of more than three figures to designate an account and other software might provide you with certain ranges that asset, liability equity, revenue or expense accounts must be allocated to according to their nature.

700 ACCOUNTING FEES

This is the account in which to record the fees that your Chartered Accountant invoices you for the annual work in preparing the financial statements and tax returns. Retainers and start up fees should also be recorded in this account. The annual work will often include consulting advice, and the preparation of returns such as the T4 and T5 returns to report salaries or dividends paid. This is an integral part of the annual work and it may be invoiced to you together in an annual invoice or as each step is completed according to your particular accountant's policy.

701 ACCOUNTING FEES - OTHER

Other accounting or bookkeeping fees should be recorded in Account 701 rather than in account 700. Include the names of the parties to whom other payments were made. This account will generally be used when you are using a bookkeeper to record your transactions. If your Chartered Accountant does your transaction recording, he may prepare a separate invoice to distinguish this work from the cost of the annual work. In that case, the payment can be recorded in this account as well.

710 ADVERTISING

Record expenses such as media advertising, gifts purchased for your clients and any expenses related to image (advertising done through your personal appearance). This includes business suits and accessories and their dry cleaning, expenses for personal grooming. Include sponsorships or donations where a tax receipt is not provided.

Caution: In an audit situation, Canada Revenue Agency will likely consider the business clothing, dry cleaning and personal grooming as personal non-deductible expenses. Based on a federal tax case and the nature of a consultant's business, I genuinely believe that in most cases these are essential business expenses for certain independent contractors. It would be prudent never the less for you to be conservative in claiming these types of expenses.

Please see the section on "Compensation for Clothing" as outlined below following the chart of expense accounts.

720 AUTOMOBILE EXPENSES

It is essential to keep a log for each vehicle used in your business indicating the total kilometers driven and the kilometers driven to earn income. Without a mileage log, Canada Revenue Agency may disallow your entire claim for the automobile. This log is essential whether you use the first method of claiming automobile expenses whereby you base the claim on your actual expenses or if you use the second method and base the claim on an allowance used for the kilometres travelled.

I advised clients to keep automobiles in their personal name to avoid taxable benefits (standby charge) being charged. While the tax cost of the benefit may be attractive if you are the recipient of a company car in another corporation; since the independent contractor pays all the costs from one pocket or another, the benefit really becomes prohibitive for his consulting company to own or lease the vehicle.

For an automobile that is owned personally, there are two options for calculating the allowable expense. It is recommended that you or preferably, your accountant does the calculation both ways each fiscal year and then claims the method which is to your advantage.

Method 1 - Based on Actual Expenses:

Calculate the percentage based on your auto log that an auto is used for business purposes to determine the amount allowable as an expense. Record each vehicle's actual expenses separately into categories such as fuel, repairs and parts, license and registration fees, insurance, general maintenance (oil changes), leasing costs (subject to a maximum – contact your Chartered Accountant's rep for the current allowable amount) and interest on auto loans. A lease down payment will be set up as a prepaid expense and amortized over the lease period. You may claim amortization on automobiles owned personally that are used in your business. Provide the market value of the car at the beginning of the first fiscal year for claiming capital cost allowance or your invoice for the purchase of the vehicle.

Provide a copy of the bill of sale for a new purchase and any details for the disposition of a vehicle that was previously being claimed.

Method 2 – A per Kilometre Allowance:

This method provides for a car allowance based on kilometers driven for business at the prescribed rates as set by Canada Revenue Agency each year. Please contact your Chartered Accountant's rep for the current allowable prescribed rates.

It is curious, but if you choose to use a rate that is different than the prescribed rates in effect at the time, it is possible that Canada Revenue Agency may deem your rate to be "unreasonable" and therefore your allowance becomes taxable in your personal tax return. Even a rate that is less than the prescribed rates can yield this assessment! You would of course be able to claim your actual expenses as a deduction against this income inclusion, however many people use this method just so they don't have to keep track of the expenses being incurred.

Both methods need to be calculated, and the one resulting in a higher expense is the one to claim. The method used may vary between vehicles if more than one is used and you can change the method used from year to year.

Lease versus buy?

One of the most common questions involving vehicles asked over the years is, "should I buy or lease a vehicle?" So, we might as well address this issue at this time.

The correct answer really depends on what you want. There are pros and cons to either scenario.

Leasing will allow you to get into a higher end vehicle with a smaller budget. You are paying for the use of the vehicle for a period of time. This time frame is generally shorter than if you were to buy the same vehicle. As such the monthly payments will be lower. My first experience with leasing was this situation. My current vehicle simply quit on me on the freeway (dangerous!!!).

After a few minutes, it restarted but the mechanic said I would have to bring it in when the car stopped operating for him to diagnose the problem. I had just test driven a Jeep Grand Cherokee a few days before. Between what I was offering for a down payment and my trade-in, the Jeep was beyond my budget. The sales manager suggested leasing the Jeep and that was the first of three Jeeps that I drove.

If you like driving a late model vehicle, leasing will help you with this as most lease terms are for about three years. This has the added value that you will be operating in a vehicle that is up to date with all the latest safety features. In recent years, I have rented vehicles and I have been amazed at how the headlights come on automatically when it gets dark. I recently rented a vehicle that can sense when there is a vehicle in the blind spot and also the wipers will start working if they sense water on the windshield! These are all new somewhat standard features that have come out since I purchased my vehicle a short five years ago.

The car that quit on me on the freeway was a comfortable vehicle that I had acquired second hand less than a year before. It was perhaps the smoothest running vehicle I have had, but it was in the shop for repairs every second month. When you lease a vehicle, you should require a minimal amount of maintenance. If things should break down, it is likely covered by warranty and you will not be paying out of pocket for repairs.

Although you are paying for the vehicle for about a three year window, that time period is when depreciation is at its greatest. You will be paying for 40% or more of the depreciation cost during those first 36 months. Another cost to consider is that you are permitted a certain number of kilometres per month in your lease. If you exceed those kilometres, you will have an end of lease assessment to pay for the excess kilometres. When I leased my first vehicle the per kilometre penalty was not very high, but the penalty rate in the contract for the third vehicle was getting pretty significant.

Your dealer will be expecting you to return the leased vehicle in near showroom condition. There is of course normal wear and tear to be expected. When I returned the last of my leased vehicles, it had a tiny scratch under the rear door handle. You had to look close to see it. I was fortunate that the dealer decided to take the vehicle back for inventory rather than pass it on to Chrysler. If they had not taken it on, they would have had to repaint the entire back door at my cost.

You generally have a lease buyout option that will allow you to buy the vehicle and perhaps resell it yourself. I still had some equity left in the first vehicle I leased when I returned it to the dealer; however for each of the next two, the vehicle was worth less than my buyout figure. In these cases, I simply handed back the keys and moved on having to come up with a deposit on the next vehicle.

On the other hand, with a purchase you generally have an asset when you have finished paying for it. You may have it paid off in four or five years. You might keep the car for five to seven years giving you several years to bank payments towards your next vehicle or to meet other critical expenses. Keep in mind that as the vehicle gets older, the warranties expire and you may have maintenance costs that you haven't anticipated. You might consider having a safety check of your vehicle just prior to the expiry of the warranty and get whatever work is needed done at that time. You may then get an extended warranty which should cover you for a reasonable period in the future should you want to retain the same vehicle for a long time.

A purchased vehicle can be sold at any time subject of course to a payout of any remaining financing. You don't have the same restrictions on selling the vehicle that you do with a lease and of course, there is no end of use fees for excess kilometres.

A lease can be written off a little faster than a purchase, if you are able to claim all or part of the costs as a business expense (based on kilometres as noted above). Over the long term, the deduction of depreciation will closely match the lease costs. There are limits on the capital cost of a vehicle that can be claimed for capital cost allowance (depreciation) purposes and there are also limits on the monthly lease amount that can be deducted. Check with your Chartered Accountant to determine the current levels of these restrictions.

Over the long term, I feel that purchasing a vehicle is the best option. It is however a personal decision.

730 BANK CHARGES

Record all bank charges from your monthly bank statements. These include costs of printing cheques, credit card annual fees and safety deposit box charges as bank transactions.

Please note that brokerage fees should be added to the cost of investments, not expensed as bank charges.

740 BOOKS AND PERIODICALS

I feel that this is one of the most overlooked expenses. It is often a spur of the moment acquisition; perhaps in the checkout line at the grocery store or the pharmacy when we are making personal purchases. We never think to keep this receipt and get reimbursed.

In this category, include costs of books, magazines, newspapers, and videos that assist you in any way with your business. The book or magazine does not have to be exclusively about your business. It may only contain one or two articles that are of value to you. Ask any man and he will tell you that he only buys Playboy magazine for the articles!

750 BUSINESS PROMOTION EXPENSE

In this category you should record 100% of all meal and entertainment expenses for actual or potential clients, as promotion expenses. Include expenses such as business meals and entertainment, including the cost of food and drink if entertaining clients at home, gratuities and cover charges, tickets to entertainment or sporting events including private boxes and room rental to provide entertainment.

Even if you are paying only for your own meal, if you are lunching with a colleague, your employer or a potential referral source, you should consider this to be a business expense. You are not simply having lunch, you are networking! Networking is the number one way that most independent contractors become aware of contracts becoming available and the best way to put them in a position that they will be in the loop when opportunities come up. Without networking, they may never know of these opportunities.

Canada Revenue Agency allows only 50% of meal and entertainment expenses to be deducted as they feel individuals are receiving some personal benefit. You should still include the full cost as a business expense. All amounts included will be reduced by 50% on the corporate tax return when your accountant reconciles between accounting income and income for tax purposes.

Golfing fees and memberships in any primarily recreational club are not tax deductible but should be recorded as a business expense as long as they serve a business purpose. Up to six "events" per year are 100% deductible if all employees are allowed to attend such as a Christmas party.

If you are considering giving gift certificates as a promotion item, keep in mind that if the certificate relates to a meal or entertainment event, it will still be subject to the 50% deductibility rule. A gift certificate for something else will not be considered for this rule. In that case, record the certificate purchase as an advertising expense rather than a promotion item.

760 COMPUTER SUPPLIES

Computer supplies would include hardware and software items costing under $200 before sales taxes. These include such items as CDs, DVDs, memory sticks, printer cartridges or toner, and printer paper. Expenditures over $200 are considered as capital assets and should be set up as such and depreciated according to their nature.

770 CONSULTING FEES

Independent contractors often require the help of others to assist with a portion of their contract or they may have multiple contracts and hire others to work some of the contracts for them. As you will be hiring them for a limited period of time and they will likely require minimal supervision, you do not need to take them on as an employee. Most often these individuals will be hired as subcontractors rather than as employees.

Record payments made to subcontractors in this account. Payments of salaries or wages to employees will be recorded in a different account (#950 – Wages and Benefits).

780 AMORTIZATION (DEPRECIATION)

Amortization is a method of writing off the cost of property, plant and equipment assets over their useful life. The amount deducted each year is generally based on the unamortized cost from the prior year. The amount and the rate at which the depreciation is calculated depends on the nature of the asset. In the case of independent contractor companies, it is often common to use the prescribed rates as set out in the Income Tax Regulations for "capital cost allowance purposes." Capital cost allowance is the tax equivalent of depreciation or amortization.

In most cases the determination and recording of the depreciation expense should be left to your accountant's staff to record. He will calculate the amortization once he has determined the value of the assets. In conjunction with this, you should probably provide your accountant with a copy of the invoice for each of the "capital" assets acquired during the year. If your accountant has that information in his file, he will be able to refer back to it when the asset is disposed of down the line. This will ensure that assets no longer owned will be properly deleted from the asset and accumulated depreciation accounts.

You should also let your accountant know about the details of any assets that have been disposed of during the fiscal year.

790 DIRECTORS FEES

Determining the amount of your annual director fees is one of the highest value functions that your accountant performs for you. If done correctly, the annual salary/dividend determination will save you tens of thousands of dollars over the years. This is more of an art than a pure science. While an objective of the exercise is to keep your taxes low, the lowest overall tax scenario may not necessarily be what is best for you. (See Chapter 10 where we discuss what you should pay yourself.)

If applicable, your accountant will record the directors' fee expense after calculation of your salary/dividend mix and allocation for the year. For the majority of independent contractors these are determined only once per fiscal year, usually at the fiscal year end with the objective to "repay" net drawings by the director(s). During the year, the contractor will take draws that are "advances against expenses." Some contractors have difficulty working in this manner as they are used to a regular monthly salary as an employee. To take advantage of the salary/dividend option and the flexibility it offers to them, they really need to learn to work with this format.

In your first fiscal year, you should consider a directors' fee in December to ensure that you are taking full advantage of the lower tax brackets and or RRSP contributions as well as a salary/dividend at your fiscal year end in the next calendar year.

800 EDUCATION AND SEMINARS

We found that the amounts being claimed for education and seminars was generally much lower than you might expect on the whole for people that are considered "knowledge–based workers". This was particularly true as most of our independent contractor clients were in the Information Technology field; an area where great and rapid changes are common-place. In discussions we found that because the changes were so frequent, by the time a course was developed, it was likely out of date. Most of the clients would compensate for this by using internet resources which were often much more current.

Few clients would take the one to three day seminars. These would represent unpaid downtime, often some travel and of course the tuition/registration fees. In many cases they would return to the office and not be able to put the new skills into practice for some time. Most of what they did learn would effectively be lost. I recently took a course in "Lightroom 4" which is post production software for retouching photographs. The instructor sent us several exercises to complete following the course. It was a stretch to recall how to do the various steps. The exercises were a great refresher. Without them it would have been like needing to learn the software all over again. I also recall my first accounting professor saying that the only way to learn accounting is to do the exercises. He was right!

I would suggest that you consider taking a course over a semester of 12 or 13 weeks. The material is then learned in slow enough periods and pace that you will retain it for a much longer period of time.

You should record costs of courses taken or seminars attended. These are courses that will assist you in your business and that do not lead to a degree or other designation that might be considered a personal benefit rather than a company expense. We generally find that courses eligible for the education and textbook claims should be paid for personally as these amounts are not available to your corporation.

A maximum of two conventions per year may be claimed provided they are business related.

810 EMPLOYEE BENEFITS

For the independent contractor this is generally only the company portion of Canada Pension Plan contributions. You should record the employer's share of CPP that you have paid during the year in this category.

Benefits such as extended health care or PHSP payments will be recorded as insurance expenses and recorded in that category rather than as a benefit.

820 GENERAL EXPENSES

There are always some things that simply do not fit into any of the other named categories. In that case, you should record any small incidental expenses that do not fit into any other category in the General Expense Account.

As a common rule, the general expense category should remain at zero, or as close to it as possible, to avoid any red flags.

830 INSURANCE

Include amounts paid for commercial insurance on buildings and equipment as well as health and dental premiums paid to a **group** plan. Individual plans are deductible as well, as long as the company pays the premiums.

Home insurance expense is claimed under the home office category as it is only a partial deduction. Vehicle insurance is similar and is claimed as an automotive expense.

Do not deduct disability premiums, as any disability benefits will then be taxable. Life insurance premiums are not tax deductible and should be paid personally.

840 INTEREST & PENALTIES

Interest paid on money borrowed to earn income is deductible.

Penalties and/or interest incurred on government remittances is not deductible for tax purposes but should be recorded for bookkeeping purposes and appropriately identified in the accounts.

Interest and penalties on taxes are generally avoidable. You should ensure that you are making any instalment payments on a timely basis. Penalties are usually only applicable if the tax return is not filed on time AND there is tax outstanding. If you can't pay your taxes on a timely basis, ensure that the return is filed on time. If it can't be filed on time, then make sure that you have provided sufficient instalments to ensure that the tax has been paid.

Don't blame your accountant if you do incur penalties or interest. Avoiding these charges is completely within your control.

850 OFFICE SUPPLIES

The majority of independent contractors will do the bulk of their work at the client's office or other worksite. They will however need to set up a home office just like any other business. Related to this is the requirement for a number of supplies. The amount will depend on how much work is done from the home office. We will often see a significant expenditure in the first year to get all the supplies setup. In subsequent years, we are usually dealing with the four "P"s, pencils, paper, printing and postage. There can be times when several major purchases (under $200 each) can make a reasonable claim, but unless you are working from your home office, supplies will be minimal.

You need to record office items such as printing, stationery, postage, delivery, paper, pens, pencils and general office supplies in this account. Office equipment or furniture costing less than $200 before sales taxes should also be included here.

860 PROFESSIONAL FEES AND MEMBERSHIPS (Dues, memberships etc.)

Record any legal or professional fees paid which may assist the Corporation in earning income in this category. The incorporation fee as well as memberships in professional and other associations should be included here.

This account is often "stretched" to include things such as Costco memberships and other similar items. As these are infrequent and usually minor in nature, we don't generally separate them into a non-professional membership's category.

870 RENT (Office in the Home)

Rent paid for property leased by the corporation, although rare, may be deducted as Rent Expense.

Clients with a home office should also record 100% of home office expenses such as heat, hydro, water, mortgage interest, home insurance, property taxes or rent, landscaping such as lawn care and snow removal, repairs and maintenance and decorating as Rent Expense.

The company pays its proportionate share of operating expenses based on square footage or ratio of rooms only. An amount based on any other criteria is considered as rent to be reported in your personal taxes and changes the usage of your principal residence. Calculate the percentage allowable by taking the amount of space used for the home office versus the total living space of the home. Do not forget to include the garage if the car is used for business.

Caution: Many clients try to claim renovations or home improvements as maintenance expenses or landscaping. These are not applicable and may affect the capital gain exemption for your principal residence.

880 REPAIRS & MAINTENANCE

Although a claim in this category is unusual you should record repairs of a strictly business nature which are not included as part of home or auto expenses in this account. This includes items such as computer and equipment repairs, and installation of electrical or telephone jacks in the office portion of the home.

890 TELEPHONE/COMMUNICATIONS

In the not too distant past, this account was referred to simply as telephone expense. Internet costs were generally from a dial up service and you generally paid by the amount of usage. That concept has fortunately faded away with internet service being high-speed and you now pay a set monthly charge according to your provider.

This account therefore is where you record expenses for cellular phones and on-line or internet services as well as long distance calls for business made from the home telephone. You should note that basic residential service is <u>not</u> deductible but a separate business line is.

As the company generally does require both internet service and a phone, the cell phone and internet are claimed 100% as a business expense. Even if these are also used for personal use, there are no marginal costs unless you exceed your allowable free air-time charges on your phone. If this should happen, you need to do an appropriate allocation of the personal portion of the usage.

900 TRAVEL

Record all business travel expenses such as plane, train, taxi, public transportation, hotel accommodations and parking. Travel expenses to attend conventions or seminars should be included here as well. You should note that the parking charges would be only business items excluding all personal parking. Do not include parking as an automotive expense.

Meals incurred while traveling are travel expenses rather than promotion expenses and should be recorded in this account as well. Please note that the meals are still only 50% deductible and any meals should be appropriately identified as 50% of the cost of them will have to be added back on the corporate income tax return.

Travel from your home office to your client's place of business would also be claimed in this account if you don't use a vehicle but take other transportation instead. This would include public transportation and car pool costs if you chip in for gas etc.

950 WAGES AND BENEFITS

Record wages paid to any employees who are not directors of the Corporation. In most cases any helpers would be hired as contractors; however you might have a need for a regular employee depending on what particular contract work you are doing. If you grow beyond the independent contractor status and become a consulting business, it is more likely for you to have one or more employees.

Clients should note that their spouse and children can be hired as employees. Any payment they receive for their services must be commensurate with the work they are doing for the company. I don't encourage paying children under the age of 14 as it may raise a question as to the viability of the work they are doing. I once had a client that wanted to pay his five year old son roughly $2,000 a year for once a week emptying the recycle bin on his computer. I quickly asked that client to find another accountant!

★ ★ ★ ★ ★ ★

COMPENSATION FOR CLOTHING

I would often inform my clients that, although I am easy to convince, I would never tell them to deduct something that I don't believe is a legitimate deductible expense. To this I would also add the caution that Canada Revenue Agency may not always agree with me. One of the more controversial items is the claim for clothing and perhaps also for certain grooming aids.

The question of deductibility of clothing and other grooming aids is an issue that I feel very strongly about. I don't feel that this issue has been given proper consideration by Canada Revenue Agency (CRA) and the courts. I am adamant that in some cases with independent contractors and others, these costs are laid out to earn income. No one will ever be able to convince me differently!

This position on the deduction of reimbursements or allowances for business clothing has been based on the premise that the expenditure is an advertising (image advertising) expense. This defense has been raised in several court cases; however I have not seen one where the court actually examined the issue before summarily rejecting it. The primary support for this position is the case of *The Queen v. Glenford R. Huffman (90DTC 6405)*.

The basic premise for deducting expenditures is that the money was laid out for the purpose of earning income from a business. The standard Canada Revenue Agency position is that the expenditure is a personal or living expense and is not deductible for the company. In addition, because it is a personal expense it is a taxable amount in the hands of the employee. "Personal or living expenses" are one of the specific exclusions from the general rule. Personal or living expenses however, are not defined in the Income Tax Act.

Many of the rulings dealing with the taxability of the clothing expenditure since the Huffman case allow that the amount is not taxable in the hands of the employee. The deduction for the corporation is however, still in doubt. I believe there is a very strong case for the amounts to be not taxable to the employee; however the case for deductibility is a tougher position to win.

Taxable Benefit:

The Huffman case was based on a plainclothes police officer being required by his contract of employment to acquire street clothes that were somewhat distinctive in nature and for which he received a $500 allowance. The allowance was held to be not taxable in his hands as he received no personal benefit from the clothes.

Revenu Quebec (IMP. 39-2) deals with compensation received by an employee for clothing. The document draws on the results of the Huffman case with the following result:

This judgment prompted the Ministère to adopt a position according to which the amounts received by an employee as reimbursement for the cost of purchasing certain street clothes the employee acquires for his employment do not constitute a taxable benefit, where all the following conditions are met:

"(a) Under his or her employment contract, the employee is required to purchase street clothes to perform his or her duties;

(b) Owing to the nature of the duties, those clothes are distinct from those the employee ordinarily wears;

(c) The cost of purchasing and caring for those clothes is reimbursed on the presentation of vouchers."

The issue of what constitutes distinct clothing is also addressed as follows:

"For the purposes of the condition described in paragraph 5(b) and article 6 above, the Ministère considers that the distinctive nature of clothing is evaluated according to its intrinsic characteristics and not according to the dress habits of the person wearing it. In other words, clothing is distinctive when it is unfit to be worn in a context other than work. For example, sober and conventional clothing that an employee is required to wear in the performance of his or her duties in order to adhere to the dress code imposed by the employer would not be considered as distinctive clothing for the purposes of 5(b) or 6 above."

However, when the context of the application of that condition or article, as the case may be, is such that the facts and circumstances are similar to those in the case of The Queen v. Glenford R. Huffman, i.e. a context in which an individual is a police officer who, in performing his duties as a plainclothes investigator, is required to purchase and wear street clothes that meet the requirements of his employer (a conservative style suit, overcoat and jacket, together with co-ordinating shirts, ties and trousers), the Ministère is prepared to be more liberal in evaluating the distinctive nature of clothing, by considering, without critical investigation, that it possesses the attributes that characterize it as such.

Thus, the ordinary business suit (and accessories) under certain conditions may be considered to be distinctive clothing.

This position is further supported by Brownlee v MNR (78 DTC 1571; 1978 CTC 2780).

In this case Brownlee (an RCMP officer) was (unsuccessfully) attempting to deduct the cost of civilian clothes required in the performance of his duties. In the findings the judge stated, "uniforms in that sense of the word cannot be so restricted as to exclude many other items of clothing, and could even include regular business suits."

I believe that Huffman and some other rulings do support the fact that allowances or reimbursement as reasonable amounts for business clothing (suits and accessories only) are not taxable to the employee and I feel fairly confident that position can be successfully argued. That is strictly my opinion and it needs to be put to the test.

Deductible Expense

The position of deductible expense is much harder to argue. The CRA position will be that the expenditure is a personal or living expense and as such is not deductible. Most claims have tried to characterize the expense as a supply. A supply, however, needs to "be consumed" during its use to be deductible. If they consider the expense to be for a "uniform," CRA and the courts will concede that the expenditure might be a class 8 addition to be depreciated at 20% a year, but will not allow it to be written off currently.

Although personal and living expenses are only very generally defined in the Income Tax Act, CRA tends to state that clothing is a personal expense, as if it is a fact, without providing any basis for that claim. We all know there are numerous expenses that are considered "personal" expenses if incurred by an employee, but are deductible business expenses if incurred by a sole proprietor or a partnership or corporation. I believe that CRA must be made to substantiate their claim based on the circumstances that the expenditure is personal.

Consider the following input on this matter:

Does the Huffman case support deductibility? The Huffman case was based on a plainclothes police officer. In this case therefore the "payer" or police department was a non profit entity that has no issue of expense/tax deductibility.

On the other hand, if Huffman had been based on say a private security agency, that company would have issues with deductibility for tax purposes. If the court decision is to be consistent, I believe the clothes would have still been a non taxable benefit to the employee, and a tax deduction to the private security agency.

Just like travel expenses can be tax benefit free to employees, but a tax deduction for the corporation employing them (providing certain criteria are met); the same concept for clothing is supported then by this case. Unfortunately, the case was not a commercial case and we don't have the other side of the coin.

The cases and rulings I have reviewed don't seem to follow this logic. It would however, seem to follow that if the employee did not receive a personal benefit from the allowance or expenditure and it is not a taxable benefit, then it is not a personal expense and should be deducted as a cost of earning the business income. There is certainly a gap in the logic which should be exploited.

Another way to look at the situation is to present it as a marginal cost concept to demonstrate that the expenditure is an expenditure laid out to earn income as follows:

As a Chartered Accountant and a partner in the firm, I wore (with rare exceptions) a suit and related accessories each and every day. Since retirement (a full year, at the time of writing) I have not worn a suit or a sports jacket even once. Most of my staff not meeting with clients would dress much more casually. The suit was therefore something that, while worn by many accountants, is not a required item of clothing. In fact, the last thing I did before leaving for work was to put on my suit. The first thing I did on arriving home at the end of the workday was to get out of the suit.

This shows that the suit is something that is not for personal use but is only for business purposes. Now consider for example that an Information Technology employee has 2 suits to get dressed up when necessary, but mostly wears casual clothes to the workplace. If that individual now becomes a contractor and gets a contract in a large formal Information Technology setting or company, those two suits would no longer suffice. He would then have to buy another 3 suits, or more, to ensure that he has a full set of suits for a 5 day work week. The additional or extra marginal cost of 3 more suits, incurred only because of obtaining the 5 day/week contract and NOT primarily for personal purposes, can be considered as a tax deductible business expense incurred to earn income. There is really no other basis for the expenditure!

If the IT contractor had not gotten the contract, or found work in a more casual work environment, he would not have had to buy the additional business suits. When the same concept has been applied to individuals working in television and movies, there have been conflicts for years, in both the United States and Canada between taxpayers and the CRA/IRS.

Although the tax authorities have rejected this concept, it is simply not a logical conclusion.

I believe in the concept fully! This argument clearly demonstrates that the expenditure is solely laid out to earn income. I think the reason it has failed is that CRA still considers the expenditure is for a "supply" rather than an advertising expense. As a minimum, they should permit the capitalization of the expenditure.

Advertising Approach

There have been a couple of cases that say kind of; "oh by the way it was an image advertising expense," however they have offered no further argument or support for this position. My personal thought is that the business suit for our consulting clients and ourselves, as accountants and other professionals for that matter is an expenditure required to provide us with a particular image. The phrase "the clothes make the man" didn't come about for no good reason at all.

To support this position, a survey by Incomm found that of 325 corporate buyers taking the survey, 72% said they were impressed by a sales agent wearing a suit. Also, Daimler-Chrysler buyer Charles Braswell has suggested that wearing a suit shows that the wearer cares about the image of his or her company and product. "When salespeople call at my office in casual attire, its not a professional image."

John Molloy wrote "Dress For Success," a book where he did extensive research on how people reacted to various clothing. When reading the book, I kept saying that his conclusions were not realistic. Then I would reflect that he has done extensive research in coming to his conclusions. His research was so extensive that he had suits broken down to colours for different occupations and colours of matching ties. This book leaves no doubt that a business suit is a powerful tool.

We can see the same thing in a courtroom. In criminal court, a defendant is always dressed in a suit rather than orange prisoner coveralls. The coveralls would scream "guilty." Or look to the judge. Would we have the same respect for the judge if he were sitting there in shorts and sandals as we do with him wearing a black robe? (Maybe he wears the shorts under the robe!). Any judge that might in future be adjudicating a case where clothing has been disallowed as a tax deduction needs to look in the mirror before entering his courtroom. To disallow the claim would be short-sighted or hypocritical at best.

Of course it always comes to a question of cost/benefit to fight. I have always recommended to my clients to be conservative in how much they claim for business suits and accessories. Even so, I had one client that annually spent and claimed over $10,000 for business clothing. Speak about her to anyone that has worked with her and they will say, "oh yes, the clotheshorse!" This client built her reputation by her clothes and her annual revenue and accumulated earnings indicate it was an excellent investment as she was one of my top three performing clients. In her case, there is no doubt that her expenditure was an effective business expense.

In most cases, since the amounts involved are usually minor compared to the costs of fighting CRA, there may never be a case fought solely or clearly on this issue alone.

Coach's Corner – A Practical Example

I am a hockey fan, however unless there is an Oilers games on, I seldom turn on the TV to watch it. The one exception is that I frequently make a point of watching the "Coach's Corner" segment between periods on CBC. I love to hear what Canada's icon coach, Don Cherry, has to say, whether I agree with him or not. Now CBC and all the other networks have commentators that I often refer to as "talking heads." This is true in sports other than hockey as well. There is not a single one of them that I would specifically turn on the TV to watch. What makes Don Cherry so different? Well he certainly has a lack of political correctness and seldom hesitates to speak his mind, but that is not what draws the fans to him. It is clearly his bombastic choice of (think drapery store, not tailor shop) apparel that makes you first notice him! I have often said that I wanted to be rich enough to afford the suits and shirts that Don Cherry wears (not that I would actually wear them). The Kingston Frontenac hockey club even produced a team sweater that mimicked one of Mr. Cherry's plaid suits!

I have no idea as to whether Mr. Cherry is an employee or an independent contractor. The point is that it is what he wears that has made him so successful. There are many "talking heads" in sports, but no one has been as successful as Mr. Cherry. There are no other "talking heads" that dress the way he does either. I personally believe there is a direct connection. It is absolutely clear that the clothes he wears are an expense laid out to earn the income that he does. If he is self-employed, his clothes are a cost of doing business!

Conclusion

I believe there is a strong case that the amounts spent on business suits and related accessories are not a taxable benefit to the employee and this point can and should be argued at both the audit and appeals level.

I fully believe that the purchase of business suits and accessories is a deductible expense under the provisions of the Income Tax Act and no one will make me believe differently, however, I am less certain about our ability to convince CRA and the courts of this position.

I believe that based on the arguments above, you would have a "defensible position" that should not attract ITA gross negligence penalties for you and/or civil penalties for your accountant. I have personally had some success in representing clients with auditors in the past.

This deduction is not really applicable to all independent contractors in all situations. For example, a contractor practicing one of the trades will have less need for a business suit than an engineer or a technology contractor. On the other hand, who would argue that a safe helmet and gloves is required and deductible by a welding contractor?

I believe contractors should continue to deduct business suits and accessories (not casual clothing), however, they should be aware that the deduction is a contentious item, that there is the possibility of double jeopardy (taxable benefit) and advise that their accountant will likely not argue beyond the appeals level. (It is unfortunate and a shame that CRA will proceed knowing this fact.) We should encourage them to be conservative with their claims such that the payment of the additional tax would not be a burden.

CHAPTER 8

Independent Contracting Risks

It Is Not All Rosy!

In 1999, George Wall of CA4IT and I jointly presented a seminar at the Edmonton Canadian Information Processing Society's annual conference held in Edmonton. The seminar was titled something like, "The Dangers of Independent Contracting." At the end of our seminar we opened the floor to questions. The first person to ask a question stated, "You seem to deal only with the benefits; I didn't hear you talk about any of the risks of independent contracting. Would you care to elaborate?" Well yes, we were busted. The seminar was presented in the period leading up to Y2K and everything had been going extremely good for independent contractors, particularly for those in the information technology sector. We were trying to sell everybody on becoming independent contractors and so naturally we approached it with rose coloured glasses and ignored the possibility that there could be a downside for the contractor.

In the interest of full disclosure therefore, I do have to admit that there are some concerns for someone looking to become an independent contractor. Some of these are beyond the control of the individual.

Clerical Maintenance

Perhaps through my entire career in working with independent contractors, the most serious concern expressed by the consultants was the pain of having to do the clerical work to track and record their income and expenses. As virtually all of my clients were incorporated entities, they had the task of recording all the revenues and expenses and tracking assets and liabilities. They need an effective way to record these transactions and keep track of the supporting documentation.

I can sympathize with my clients; however I did encourage them all to do their own bookkeeping rather than farming it out to a bookkeeper or asking my firm to record the individual transactions. In most cases the bookkeeping task would fall to the spouse of the contractor. This did provide a basis for paying remuneration to a spouse as his/her contribution to the operation of the business. I made this recommendation to do their own bookkeeping to my clients based on personal experience. At one point I used to record all the banking and credit card transactions for my firm. When I was doing this, I had full knowledge of where we stood with respect to revenues and expenses. I knew when certain payments would be due and approximately how much we were looking at for each expense. As my practice began to grow fairly rapidly, this task became too much for me to handle. In fact, I was almost a full year late in filing my own corporate tax return for one year. I was very fortunate in that my wife Linda is a well experienced bookkeeper. She was able to take over this function for me. The downside of designating these duties is that from that point forward I did not have a good handle on the day to day expenses. I would sit down at year end to prepare my annual financial statement and constantly be surprised at how much we had spent in various expense categories.

I still had a handle on the revenues that were being generated as these were recorded through a separate accounting system.

Looking after all the record-keeping can be bothersome however, the ultimate rewards are well worth the nuisance caused by this extra administrative work.

Technological Changes

The makers of buggy whips are pretty much out of business these days. So too, are the makers of eight track tape players and Beta recording tapes as these items have become extinct. More recently, one of the major players in producing photographic film has fallen on hard times with the advent of digital cameras.

There are several factors that affect the marketplace for independent contractors depending on what industry they might be in. It has been my take that consultants working in the information technology sector are extremely susceptible to the introduction or lack thereof of technological changes. Contractors in the trades, technology sectors and engineers are perhaps more susceptible to the ups and downs of the economy.

Back in the late 1990s, the information technology sector was growing at an exponential rate. As a result of this growth, it became a primary time for people with IT skills to venture to become independent contractors. It may not be well-known, but even when we reached Y2K and any major disasters were averted, the information technology sector continued to grow and add jobs on an annual basis. The anticipated rate of growth, however, did not materialize and even though the industry experienced net gains, the slowdown in the rate of growth resulted in numerous layoffs. Students leaving community colleges and university with training in IT were finding it difficult to obtain employment. The problem was further exasperated because there were few if any new major innovations in the early days of the new century.

A number of my clients in the information technology sector had their expertise in the older legacy computer systems. For them, it was a matter of how you looked at opportunities. While there were fewer new positions open, the legacy systems were not going away and no one was being trained in how to use them. As long as they were able to maintain their expertise, they were generally assured of continued employment, although their opportunities for change were greatly restricted.

Although I have indicated that technologists and engineers are less affected by technological change than information technology consultants are, they are not exempt from the influence of this factor. As I was retiring, I'm aware that one of my clients was heavily involved in new technological advancements to address the pollution issues with the tailing ponds created through the oilsands extraction process. Technological changes he was involved in produced considerable work for himself and his co-investors and may influence the ongoing work of his peers.

Economic Change

Independent contractors in the information technology sector are primarily affected by technological changes. They are not however completely exempt from changes in economics as well. As companies fall on hard times they may be prone to cut back on their technology expenditures. This is likely a recipe for disaster as staying at the forefront of technology is imperative to remain competitive. Even when cutbacks are made, they are not generally very deep or long lasting.

I look back at moving my family from Kingston, Ontario to Edmonton in late 1978. Kingston and Ontario in general at the time was fairly stagnant while Alberta was in the midst of an oil and gas boom. The national accounting firm I worked for in Kingston was hoping that staff would leave in order to make room for new people to move upwards. Calgary and Edmonton on the other hand were begging for warm bodies. The managing partner in Kingston called his counterpart in Edmonton and they arranged for me to fly out for a day and a half of interviews. Although the offer made to me was not something that I couldn't refuse, the economy out west was so much more robust than what was happening in Ontario that my wife and I decided to engage in a new adventure. It was the relative state of the economy between the two provinces that made my decision for me. Although Mr. Trudeau's National Energy Program, introduced a couple of years after we arrived in Edmonton, put the Western economy in the tank for the next decade, we decided to stay.

Engineers, technologists and trades contractors are much more affected by economic instability. Through most of 2008 and 2009 my Calgary partner and I developed an Association with a placement firm working out of Calgary. This placement firm was recruiting engineers and engineering technologists from all around the world. Somehow they had learned that we specialized in working with independent contractors and they made all the referrals exclusively to myself or my partner in Calgary. With the huge number of referrals coming from this one source, I tended to ignore my marketing efforts in other areas. As everyone is aware, between the end of August 2009 and the middle of September 2009 the world economy experienced a bit of a meltdown that affected pretty much everyone. With this unexpected slowdown, many of our new clients in Calgary were laid off immediately. To their credit, the Edmonton engineering firm that was hiring most of the referrals coming from the Calgary placement firm, tried to keep the contractors working as long as they could. At one point I would estimate that approximately 80% of the recent hires were laid off. These were people that have given up their home in another country to come to Canada only to find themselves without work and no employment insurance to support them.

While many of our clients packed up and returned to their home country, almost all those who remained in Canada were rehired as soon as the economy picked up again. At this point, however, the engineering firm was offering full-time employment rather than a contracting position to most of our clients. It is not hard to understand, given the circumstances they had just gone through, but a good number of our clients opted to take an employment position.

Financial Uncertainty

Whether the economy is good or bad, there is always a degree of security that comes with receiving a corporate paycheque. For an individual considering contracting, this may not be a significant concern, however for anyone supporting a family, it can be nerve-racking. It does help if your spouse is employed, and you have at least some income to see you through.

Before you take the steps to become an independent contractor, it might be wise to visit your bank and apply for as large a line of credit as you can get. Your banker will be basing your credit worthiness on your employment record of recent years. It is quite typical that an independent contractor will find it difficult to get a line of credit or to secure a mortgage if he is looking to buy a new home. There are few bankers that understand business and particularly independent contracting. They will want to see what your T4 slip (Employment Income) indicates your income to be. With prudent financial planning in mind, independent contractors would be encouraged to minimize their personal income and leave assets (cash) in the Corporation to be taxed at the low corporate tax rates. So while you may be netting 60 to 80% more after taxes than a full time employee, as a contractor you will have a much harder time qualifying for a mortgage. What is even more telling is that such a corporation will actually be paying a portion of that mortgage interest as one of the factors in determining the office in the home cost.

Whether you are an employee or an independent contractor, it is all too easy to become comfortable with your work and the income flow that you are receiving as a result. This can all change in a hurry. A change in top management, budgetary changes or even the successful completion of your assigned project can result in the termination of your contract and you find yourself looking for a new one. The anticipated end of the contract is something that should spur you to be taking action towards finding new work, however, some of the other issues may catch you by surprise. If you haven't been doing your homework and maintaining your network, it could be like starting your business all over again. It is only by staying on top of your business that you will find new projects to keep you afloat.

While it might be ideal for one contract to end and a new one to start with perhaps a one or two week break between, this does not always happen. It becomes essential for the independent contractor to manage his cash flow and set aside funds to see him/her through extended gaps between contracts. As being in a position to select the work that you want to do is one of the major benefits of independent contracting, you do need to properly manage your cash. This will enable you to wait for the type of contract work that you really want to do.

To undertake independent contracting, the individual must have sufficient self-confidence in their personal skills to see it through. Most of the issues surrounding financial uncertainty can be dealt with whether the economy is good or bad. In the world of sailing the saying goes that you cannot direct the wind, but you can adjust your sails.

Health Insurance Concerns

I recall that whenever I changed jobs, I was a little concerned that my new employer would have a health plan that was comparable to what I was leaving behind. At the time, I found my concern to be a little strange because when we started out my wife had a benefit plan that included dental coverage. We quickly determined that her contribution to the benefit plan far exceeded what the two of us were paying for dental care. Further, it was not until I was working for my fourth employer that we even thought to make a claim for prescription drugs even though we had the coverage.

Many of my clients shared a concern about losing the health insurance benefits that they held with their current employer should they make the decision to become an independent contractor.

When I started working with independent contractors, I presented numerous seminars on the advantages of independent contracting. I was fortunate enough to have Brenda Douglas from HDF Financial in Edmonton to present with me. Brenda is the national broker for the Canadian Information Processing Society and through that association; she has developed insurance and benefit programs designed specifically for the independent contractor. It was through her presentations that both my clients and I learned that the insurance and benefit packages can be economically replaced.

During the summer of 2009, my second son, Matt, was considering becoming an independent contractor through the installation and maintenance of overhead doors. Fortunately, his negotiation broke down in early September 2009 when the company reneged on their agreement to sell him the company truck he had been using. As you know from our discussion above, the economy collapsed a couple of weeks later. That issue, along with his injuring a knee and requiring surgery, would have been disastrous if he had followed through. The timing of all of this was such that the company found work for him to do around the shop, he had his surgery and recovery covered by the health benefit plan in place at the time.

Whenever you change a job, whether it is to become a contractor or to continue as an employee, there may be a waiting period before new coverage comes into effect. Whether you are a contractor or an employee, you will be at risk during this period. Nevertheless, there are both benefits and insurance packages available at a reasonable rate to replace the benefits you are leaving behind.

Learning New Skill Sets

Technical competence and a great economy still are not a guarantee of success as an independent contractor. Beyond the technical knowledge and skills that you need for your particular industry segment, there are a number of other skills that you will need to take on yourself. In the corporate environment, there are likely separate departments to assist you in carrying out various aspects of your project. As an independent contractor, you will not have the luxury of being able to delegate a number of tasks. As such, you will have to deal with your own computer literacy (assuming you are not an IT consultant), marketing and sales of your services and writing reports or giving presentations. You'll also need to be concerned about the management of your money as well as your time.

Not everyone will be adept at these various skills, at least when they start out. Many of them will be adapted through a period of trial and error. I know for myself in trying to operate an accounting practice, there were a number of things that I learned simply by doing and assessing the results, and determining what I might do differently next time.

Personal Service Business Risk

One of the major concerns in operating as an independent contractor comes from Canada Revenue Agency. While you may feel that you are operating as an independent contractor, the government may have a different opinion.

In previous chapters, I have alluded to the concern about your business being declared a personal service business (PSB). Should Canada Revenue Agency assess your business as a personal service business, you would be denied any and all deductions claimed by your corporation other than those that would be allowed to a full-time employee. This essentially means your salary and perhaps a car allowance would be all that would be allowable as deductible expenses. Recent legislation regarding PSBs eliminates the general rate reduction on federal tax making the PSB tax rate about 13% more than the general corporate tax rate. The corporate tax alone will approximate the tax payable on a salary in the hands of an employee. If you then add the tax payable on a dividend to remove the income from the company, the tax through a PSB is much higher than that earned by an employee.

Let me be perfectly clear. An independent contractor is not a personal service business! The risk comes in having Canada Revenue Agency declare your independent contractor business as a personal services business. The problem is that Canada Revenue Agency and its personnel are not held to any level of accountability for their actions. In a recent Federal Court of Appeal (FCA) case (Ereiser v. The Queen) the FCA concluded that even if an auditor acts outside of documented guidelines and authority, an assessment or reassessment is subject to the same process for appeal as any other assessment. This conclusion came despite that fact it was clear that the assessment arose as the result of a "flawed" audit and process!

The FCA did comment in the Ereiser case that the taxpayer may have the right to sue for damages through other courts. The only options for a taxpayer unfortunately are to incur additional accounting and legal fees as well as lost time to challenge the reassessment or to live with the reassessment and pay up. A taxpayer could sue through small claims court to a maximum of $25,000 and handle the suit by themselves. The taxpayer would be challenged with proving that the government was negligent in the matter. You probably would not be surprised if I tell you that some of the case law to date has held that auditors do not have a duty of care to the taxpayers that they audit.

As mentioned previously, the football coach, Ralph Sazio's actions in incorporating to provide his services lead directly to the creation of the personal service business tax rules. It wasn't until the mid eighties when the Wiebe Door case lead to the codification of four tests to distinguish an independent contractor from a personal service business. Stemming from the Wiebe Door case, there are certain criteria that distinguish an independent contractor from an employee. In order to be considered as a contractor, you must meet a weighted average of the various subjective issues to avoid a classification as an employee. We will have a closer look at some of these criteria below. In my experience, Canada Revenue Agency auditors and appeals officers will look over these criteria to find like concerns and then proceed to completely ignore those concerns that support the contention that the entity is not a PSB.

It is best to start with some definitions so that everyone is on the same wavelength before we get too far into the subject.

Definitions:

Employee – *a contract of service.*

Independent Contractor – *a contract for services.*

Personal Service Corporation – *a situation where the worker would be an employee except for the existence of the corporation.*

In practice, a Canada Revenue Agency auditor could be looking at two birds floating on a pond. He will consider that both birds have feathers and a beak and wings and they both have webbed feet. He will then conclude that based on these observations, he is looking at two ducks. He will not give any consideration to issues that might oppose his conclusion. You can point out that the second bird is much bigger than a duck, its feathers are pink rather than browns and greens, the beak is curved, the birds emit different sounds and therefore it cannot be a duck. In fact it is often referred to as a flamingo rather than a duck. If you point out these discrepancies, the auditor will respond that those issues are not relevant and the bird will be declared to be a duck. If you don't agree then by all means exercise your right to spend all kinds of money on an appeal that might get an appeals officer to agree that it might be a flamingo like duck. This analysis may sound a little farfetched. Unfortunately there is too much truth in how it compares to the way that many auditors will end up with their assessment. While I would prefer to think this is because of gross incompetence, there is overwhelming evidence in recent actions that it is part of a CRA assessment practice in at least one regional office.

In recent years, the upper tax courts and the Supreme Court of Canada have indicated that the intention of the parties is a significant criterion in determining whether or not a business is that of an independent contractor or can be considered a personal service business. To document the intention of both parties to an independent contractor agreement, it would be wise to put the mutual intentions in writing.

Preparing a written contract:

In recent years the number of contract jobs for the knowledge-based worker has increased substantially. Many of these contracts are for office jobs for individuals where they perform work side-by-side with full-time employees, although they don't receive the same benefits. In recent years, labor shortages have also extended the need to allow more contract work being done in the trades; particularly in Alberta.

As an employee, you are sheltered by a myriad of labour laws that offer you protection in your employment position. The same labour laws that govern employment relationships do not protect contract workers. These workers rely on the contracts they sign to ensure they are fairly treated.

A written contract has become extremely important. In relatively few cases, an employee requires a written agreement; however a written contract becomes a necessity when the payer and the worker want to establish an independent contractor relationship. The contract is important, not only to protect the rights of these workers, but to ensure that Canada Revenue Agency does regard them as independent workers, as opposed to employees.

A review of jurisprudence since 2000 indicates that a written contract can be an important factor in the determination of whether a worker is an employee or an independent contractor. From the mid-1980s, the courts have held that to be an independent contractor, you must meet the tests as set out in the 1986 Wiebe Door case.

These criteria form a four-in-one test to be considered together in a subjective weighting:

1. *Control Test* – Who controls the work? Can the employer tell you what to do, versus how to do it?
2. *Ownership Of Tools Test* – Who owns or supplies the tools?
3. *Chance Of Profit or Loss Test* – Is any risk being assumed by the contractor?
4. *Integration Test* – How closely integrated is the worker's business to the employer's.

Until about 2000, the above tests constituted the basis on which the courts decided whether or not a worker is an employee or an independent contractor. If the worker has incorporated his business, the same criteria are applied to determine if the relationship is that of an independent contractor or a personal service business.

Since 2000, the courts have essentially said:

"Unless the actual actions of the parties strongly contradict the intentions of the parties as stated in a written contract, and/or some element of deceit is present, "the authorities" (CRA) should respect the choice made by the parties in a written contract."

It is important that in a written contract, the parties state whether or not their relationship is that of an employment relationship or an independent contractor relationship. In front of the courts, the contract will be given weight only if it actually reflects the relationship that exists between the worker and the payer. Substance over form is still extremely important. Where the facts do not point to an employment or independent contractor relationship, the express intention of the parties with respect to the nature of their relationship becomes much more important as the courts will tend to give a greater weight to the express intentions in the contract.

We will be going through each of the four major criterion used by the courts but it is important to consider the definition of personal service business. As noted above, a personal service business or corporation represents "a situation where the worker would be an employee except for the existence of the corporation." Consider that we went through three separate chapters of this book outlining the benefits of independent contracting for both the worker and the payer. Given the enormous mutual benefit of an employer and a contractor entering into an independent contractor agreement is overwhelming; it would be an extremely rare situation where the actions of the parties to the agreement under the other four criteria contradicted the intentions of the parties to such an extent that some element of deceit or fraud would be present. This is not to say that an issue of deceit or fraud would not exist, but it does raise the bar that Canada Revenue Agency should be required to meet in applying these criteria. The criteria are subject to a subjective weighting and based on a mutual intention to enter into an independent contracting agreement, any inadvertent breaching of the other tests should not outweigh the intention of the parties.

The Control Test

Although the Wiebe Door criteria are set as a four-in-one test where all the tests are to be considered together and given a subjective weighting, the control test has perhaps been relied on to a greater extent than the other criteria. This test looks at the extent to which the payer controls the activity of the worker.

Normally, an independent contractor is hired because they possess some specific knowledge or skill. They are hired to achieve a particular result through the application of their knowledge or skill. If the payer wants to tell the contractor not only what needs to be done, but also how to do it, then a control problem likely exists. The contract should clearly identify the work that is required resulting in a goal-specific relationship. Having said this, one can see that it would not be appropriate for the payer to train the worker, if it is at all possible.

The contract should set out all the important terms of the relationship, particularly those factors that are important to the characterization of the arrangement. Particularly with respect to the control test, the contracts should expressly provide that the worker:

A. can set his/her own hours;

B. is not required to perform the services at the location of the hirer's business if circumstances would otherwise permit:

C. is subject to minimal supervision and minimal reporting requirements;

D. is entitled to hire and pay for assistants to do the work in his place; and

E. is not restricted from working for entities other than the hirer.

It is very important that the wording of a contract be set out in a "can do" fashion rather than a restrictive way. For example; the entitlement to hire and pay for assistants to do the work in his place should be set out in a way that clearly indicates this can be done. There might be approvals and other considerations that allow the payer to ensure that any replacement has the required skills and is qualified to do the work.

The relationship between the payer and an independent contractor should not be much different than their relationship between my firm and my clients. A client would hire my firm and perhaps I would do a portion of the work, but it would be up to me to determine who does the detail work and how it is done.

It should also be considered that the written agreement sets out the entire agreement between the contractor and the payer. If the payer requests that the contractor do something not covered by the agreement, (i.e. meeting with employees at specified times to coordinate activities) it is a "gentleman's request" only. The payer is not exercising control as the contractor has the right to refuse since it is not a requirement in the contract. The contractor has the right to assess whether or not the request will aid him in fulfilling his contract. If he deems it so, he will agree to the meetings, however this should never be confused as the payer exercising any kind of control!

In many cases, a contractor's company is owned at least in part by a spouse. Remember that it is the company and not the individual that has entered into the contract relationship. Even if some degree of control can be exercised over the on the job worker, the corporation likely cannot be controlled by the payer. Under this criterion, the control question should relate to the entity that holds the contract and not simply to the particular worker. This disconnect has not been considered by CRA and the courts, yet it seems to be a pretty basic oversight that the worker is not a direct party to the legal relationship.

Ownership of Tools Test

The second test from the Wiebe Door case suggests that you need to also consider whether or not the worker must supply his own tools in the completion of his work. If specific tools are required, it is important that the worker's requirement to supply his or her own tools should be considered when establishing the contract. In most cases, particularly where the contractor is an IT consultant, the tendency is to use the employer's computers and office equipment. While conducting the work in these cases, it should be noted that the contractor should also own his own computer, telephone and office equipment that allows him to do his own record-keeping and to do research. Clients don't normally allow you to do your bookkeeping on their computers.

Where practical, rather than the client leasing a truck to be used by the worker or providing a computer that can be used by the worker, the payer and worker should consider having the worker lease the equipment and attempt to adjust the remuneration to reflect the added cost. The workers should also be responsible for the maintenance of that same equipment as well as have their own insurance policy.

Although, the courts have not expressly acknowledged it, the major tool that a knowledge-based worker brings to the job is his specialized skills. He is hired specifically for those skills and his knowledge, and as such, they are major tools that the worker brings to the engagement. The courts in some cases have recognized that the ownership of tools is really a non-issue when it would not matter whether the worker was an employee or a contractor. This would apply where for example the payer's tools (e.g. computers) must be used because of a security issue.

Therefore the contractor should have his own website, business cards, an independent address and phone number. He should indicate his own corporate name in the signature of all emails, including those sent from his client's workplace.

Chance of Profit or Loss

The remuneration of an independent contractor must be determined in a way much different from that of an employee. To the extent possible, the contract should reflect a chance of profit or loss. The contract for an independent contractor should address the following considerations:

- Although most contracts are set for an hourly fee, where possible, the contract should set up a fixed fee for specified results.
- It is important that the worker is not provided with benefits that are provided to employees of the client. For example, health plans, stock options, etc.
- The worker should be required to invoice the payer for work done, rather than simply submitting a timesheet. It should set out that the contractor is responsible for maintaining his own books and records.
- The contract should specify that the worker be required to pay all income taxes, Goods and Services taxes and Canada Pension Plan contributions personally, as opposed to having the client remit payments on behalf of the independent contractor.
- The contract should specify that the contractor is responsible for his own insurance coverage including, where applicable, WCB coverage, general liability and professional liability insurance.

- If applicable, the contract should establish the worker's responsibility for bad debts.
- When additional remuneration is established for the worker to supply tools and the maintenance thereof, such remuneration should not be on a dollar for dollar basis, but should simply acknowledge these costs are an extra fee. The actual costs may be more or less, establishing a chance for profit or risk of loss.

Contracts should establish that the contractor has a liability to the client for the work done. There should be an obligation to do warranty work at his or her expense. There should also be a responsibility for damages to the payer's equipment or materials.

It is important that the contractor appears to be "in business." This entails such things as being responsible for one's own bad debts, having one's own business cards and email address.

Integration Test

Whose business is it? In an employee/employer relationship, a worker is employed as part of that business. The services provided by an employee are an *integral* part of that business. On the other hand, an independent contractor is not integrated into that business, but is merely *ancillary* to it.

The courts have in many cases misapplied this test. There are two methods of applying this test; one is from the perspective of the employee and one, from the perspective of the employer. In virtually any case applying the test from the perspective of the employer it will prove that the individual is integral to the operation of the employer. When properly approached from the persona of the contractor, the test provides fairer results.

To avoid being caught by this test, the contract should specify that the contractor has the right to work for other entities and thereby demonstrating that the employer is not crucial to the survival of the contractor. All contracts should be drawn up for a specified period of time. New contracts should be signed upon maturity of the original contract.

Making the Move

Often, after working for an employer for some time, an employee will want to become an independent contractor to take advantage of the substantial financial benefits and non-financial advantages available. In such circumstances, it is extremely important to dot the 'i's and cross the 't's. There must be a noticeable and recognizable change in the status of the employee.

Canada Revenue Agency has indicated the following:

"We have concerns with those situations where individuals, for all intents and purposes, will provide almost the same if not the same services under the conditions to an employer, but will have a different employment status."

Under these circumstances it becomes even more imperative to have a properly worded contract in place before the commencement of the change in status if staying with the same payer.

Other Considerations

The above comments are centred primarily on ensuring that the contractor is viewed as such and not looked at as being an employee. Most employers insist on independent contractors being incorporated to protect them from the consequences of having Canada Revenue Agency assess the relationship as that of an employer/employee.

In practice, most contractors either do not have a written contract or they blindly accept the contract presented by the hiring company (including employment agency contracts) and generally do not have them reviewed by a lawyer. Lawyers typically charge between $400 and $1,500 to review a contract. Many contractors feel this is too much. It can be a worthwhile expense at least on your first contract giving you a feel for what should be in the contract as well as what should not be in there. Keep in mind that most lawyers will do a good job of examining the clauses that the hiring company puts in the contract and some will look for the concerns raised above with respect to the contractor/employee concerns, however, they may not raise concerns about other clauses that might be beneficial to the contractor, particularly if those clauses have not already been addressed in the contract.

After reviewing a number of contracts put out by placement firms, I would strongly recommend that an independent contractor should review such a contract in great detail. My associates and I have found that some of the worst contracts are those used by the placement firms. In many cases, they actually state "contract of employment" or referred to other terms associated with employees, such as "payroll."

Some of the major items to keep in mind when signing a contract are as follows:

Elements of a Good Contract

Fees and Payment Terms:

The actual fees to be paid and when they are payable may seem very basic to any contract although these terms are often left out. These matters must be clearly stated in the contract. It should lay out the frequency for the issuance of invoices and the deadline for the payment of those invoices. There should also be provision for charging interest on delinquent payments.

If these matters are not specified in the contract, you may find that the client will delay payment for months, particularly if there is any dispute over the services rendered.

Nature (Mandate) of the Agreement:

As was mentioned above, a contractor is hired to provide a specific service. Your contract should very clearly specify what work you are expected to do. This helps protect you with the contractor/

employee position, however, it also protects you from a company reneging on its obligation to pay you by stating that the services they hired you for have not been delivered or alternatively not delivered in a satisfactory manner.

Coverage of Expenses:

It will vary from industry to industry and the nature of your contracting services (eg IT consulting versus millwright services) as to what expenses the payor company will be willing to cover. If the company promises to pay for certain expenses then they should be clearly identified in the contract as well as the terms of payment.

For accounting purposes, you should be able to identify if these are reimbursements of specific expenses or an allowance. This will determine if it is your expense or that of your "client."

An "allowance" means any pre-determined amount of money that an individual/contractor receives from an employer/payer, in addition to salary, wages or contract fees, without having to account for its use. The amount of the allowance and the amount of the expenses incurred by the individual/contractor do not necessarily correspond, nor is there necessarily correspondence between the expenses covered by the allowance and the actual expenses incurred.

A "reimbursement of expenses" means an amount of money which an employer/payer pays to an employee/contractor on proof that expenses have been incurred. The reimbursement may be total if it covers all the employees/contractor's expenses or partial if it covers only certain expenses. There is always an exact correspondence between the expenses incurred and the amount reimbursed, since the reimbursement is made after the expenses have been incurred.

Minimum Charges:

Some contracts are flat fee or based on a materials used calculation, however, most contracts are structured on an hourly basis. The structure will vary by the nature of the work that you are doing or by the industry that you are involved in. One downside of the hourly basis from the contractor's standpoint is that the payer can use you on an as needed basis. If no work is available, then the organization does not need to pay you. This arrangement is a major benefit to the employer to use independent contractors.

If you are on an hourly-based contract, you should consider negotiating a retainer or minimum payment. For those who are "on call" a minimum three-hour charge for any on-site client work would be reasonable to cover the inconvenience of your travel time and just being "available." You might even negotiate a fee for simply being on call even if not called upon for the inconvenience of making yourself available.

Intellectual Property:

The ownership of intellectual property is an important factor for contractors, particularly those in the IT industry. Under an employment relationship, it is quite clear that the employer owns the intellectual property (product or invention created by the employee). The employee cannot take that creation and use it elsewhere. The rules under a contract relationship are not as clear-cut and so it is imperative that the contract specifies who owns the intellectual property. If you want to retain ownership or use the work you have done for the benefit of other clients, it is important for the contract to specify who owns what.

In some cases, the contractor will be making use of proprietary information or property that the client has already developed. The contract should lay out the need for confidentiality and use and ownership of this intellectual property.

Length of the Contract and Early Termination:

Most contracts will specify the term of the contract whether it is for three months or two years. An open-ended contract may not be enforceable. The problems arise when either the contractor or the payer wants to end the contract before the specified termination period has expired. It is a good idea to have a minimum notice period for cancellation for both parties to the contract. Many contracts contain penalty clauses for early termination.

Non-Competition Clauses:

Some contracts contain clauses that prevent you from accepting a contract with a competitor for a certain period of time. It is difficult to assess how the courts will look upon such clauses. They are normally opposed to clauses that place an unfair restriction on you; however, they also acknowledge that you entered into the agreement fully aware that the non-competition clause may restrict your ability to earn a living. If the clause restricts your ability to find work within too large a geographical area or for too long a period of time, it is possible the courts will find in favour of the contractor. If the terms are reasonable, they will more likely find in favour of the client.

The restrictions will vary from one industry to another, so it is important to understand what the norm is in your particular industry. If you find your contracts through a placement firm, you will likely find a non-competition clause in their agreement specifying that you can't work for that particular client (as either an employee or a contractor), except through the placement firm.

<u>Contract First – Work Later:</u>

A recent tax court case brought out the need to have the contract in place before you commence work. In this case a contract was drawn up a few months after the contractor had started working. He and the payer drew up the contract to confirm the arrangements; however the courts sided with Canada Revenue Agency and declared the contractor to have been an employee because the contract was not in place when the agreement started.

From the contractor standpoint, you should consider that you lose some negotiating power if you start work before the contract is in place. While you don't want to risk losing an opportunity, it may be wise to ensure that details are worked out first. You are looking to achieve a mutually satisfactory arrangement.

Caution

Despite all that has been said with respect to the intentions of the parties and everything related to the preparation and wording that goes into a written agreement, Canada Revenue Agency may simply ignore all these factors. They will assess your company as a personal service business regardless of the steps you have taken to ensure that your relationship is designated as that of an independent contractor. In 2009/10, the Shawinigan–Sud Tax Centre located in Quebec began to assess numerous independent contractors as personal services businesses.

Two clients in our Ottawa office were reassessed by this "campaign." One of these clients had actually contracted to Revenue Canada during the period under assessment! I had firsthand knowledge of the details as I wrote the response to the auditor for one of these clients and the Notice of Objection for both of them, on behalf of our Ottawa office. I also assisted our Toronto office in submitting the response to the auditor for the other client. I can't elaborate on the details of why CRA felt the companies were personal service businesses for confidentiality reasons. The issues have been covered generically in the material in this chapter.

I was absolutely appalled at the response we received from the auditor to whom I had written the appeal. She stated that, the intention of the parties was "not relevant." She proceeded to indicate that their position was based on a particular court case. This case was one decided under Quebec civil law which has no standing throughout the rest of Canada. The decision in that particular case was being used as a precedent and yet the actual decision was really questionable when considered under the Wiebe Door criteria.

There were only two issues that might give rise to Canada Revenue Agency continuing with their assessment. The first is that the auditor was grossly incompetent. I discount this position as her assessment would have to be reviewed and approved by a supervisor. The other concern is that Canada Revenue Agency was conducting a campaign with the hope that the taxpayers would simply pay the assessments instead of incurring the time and expense of fighting it. I didn't charge our Ottawa office for the work I did on these assessments, however on the market, the value of that service would have been about $5,000 or more for each client. Canada Revenue Agency knows that most taxpayers will pay the assessment rather than incur that cost just to launch an appeal. If the client was to take the issue to court, they might be looking at tens of thousands of dollars to carry the fight to the upper courts.

The determination of a personal service business (PSB) is based on criteria set out by the courts. In their audit proposal letter, the auditor set out the legislation, but the courts have set out how that legislation is to be interpreted. The Wiebe Door tax case in 1986 was a landmark case in that it established four basic criteria to be considered in determining whether or not an individual was operating as an independent contractor or as an employee.

While there are only four criteria; within each of those criteria there are numerous issues to be considered. In addition, Canada Revenue Agency cannot rely on simply one or two issues within each criterion. The courts have clarified that it is clearly a four in one test. In reaching their conclusion that the taxpayer is a PSB, they put forward only a few issues and did not consider any conflicting issues. In Canada, you do not have to be onside with all the issues and the end result is reached through a subjective weighting of all the numerous criteria. It was apparent from their letter that they had failed to properly consider all the issues in play before concluding that the taxpayer is a PSB. Some of the issues they were relying on for their assessment were not accurate as clearly laid out in the written contracts.

The statement that the intention of the parties was not relevant was particularly disconcerting. Since 2000, the upper courts have given a lot of weight with respect to a further criterion to be considered. That criterion is "What was the intent of the parties to the contract?" The courts have essentially stated that where a written contract exists and barring any consideration of sham or fraud, that Canada Revenue Agency must honour the terms of that contract. In the case of our clients, there existed written contracts, the contracts expressed unequivocally that the nature of the relationship was that of a contract for service with an independent contractor. The contracts had been conducted such that there can be no consideration of fraud or sham. Keep in mind that one of the contracts under review was with Canada Revenue Agency itself. As such, CRA should have been compelled to honour the contracts as they were written.

From my point of view, the conduct of Canada Revenue Agency in this campaign was less than honorable. Do they really want us to believe that one department of a government agency is saying that their own organization is complicit in a fraud or sham? At the date of writing, I don't know the results of our client's objections.

Despite the above noted action of the Shawinigan-Sud Tax Centre, the assessment of an independent contractor as a personal service business or an employee (for sole proprietors) is relatively rare. The above campaign by Shawinigan-Sud was the most serious federal approach I am aware of in fifteen years of working with contractors, but the issue was isolated to that Tax Centre. In the early 2000s, the Mississauga office of Revenue Canada did a "campaign" as well. Although it was short-lived, a couple of clients in the Toronto office of "CA4IT" were caught in the initial rush.

In Edmonton, the issue has only come up with one of my clients. It was actually before he became a client. He was advised by an auditor that, except that he was about to wind up his company, the auditor would assess his company as a personal service business. Well, the taxpayer didn't wind up his company. Instead, he obtained a new contract after his audit and came to me to look after his accounting and tax needs. We continued to reflect his company as an independent contractor and he experienced no further issues with it being declared a personal service business. He met all the relevant criteria of an independent contractor!

Canada Revenue Agency is not the only taxing authority in Canada that has targeted independent contractors with respect to the personal service business issue. Commencing in about 2006, independent contractors in the IT sector in Quebec have suffered from a campaign by the Quebec government (Revenu Quebec). Their companies, operating under computing subcontracts have had their earnings assessed as earnings coming from a personal service business as the result of a host of tax audits by the authorities.

In response, The Quebec Association of IT Freelancers (AQIII) took up the torch and funded the appeals of a couple of the members that had been assessed as PSBs. In June of 2011, they were rewarded with a positive court decision with respect to T.A.P. Consultant Inc. The case, which involved a taxation dispute between the company and Revenu Quebec, ruled that the taxpayer was not a personal service business as the government had claimed, but rather was an active business that was eligible for the small business deduction.

Later in the fall of 2011, they (AQIII) were successful again with another win in court. In this case, the company Pragma Services Conseils Inc. was also deemed by the courts to not be a personal service business. In addition, the ruling addressed the problems of the independent contractor not having multiple clients and/or working for one client for an extended period of time. The judgement determined that the contractor status is not according to the number of clients served or the duration of assignment with a particular client, but rather determining the deliverables, the specific mandates and the intended duration of the parts. It is important to point out that the independent professional needs to remain vigilant. Although the case was in Quebec and may not hold much influence in the rest of Canada, the judge did point out specific criteria. You need to avoid any relationship of subordination and you need to use a good contract.

(The Quebec Association of IT Freelancers (AQIII) is a private non-profit association of more than 1,400 self-employed independent IT contractors. It facilitates the availability of IT mandates, networking, and the sharing of information among IT consultants and access to discounts with specific suppliers.)

The above points out that it is important even with a written contract to walk the walk of being an independent contractor. The benefits and trappings that are specifically designed for employees should be shunned. This is still no guarantee that Revenue Canada auditors will honour your commitment to the way you intend to conduct your relationship with your client.

★ ★ ★ ★ ★

A Sample Contract

As indicated in the caveat in the introduction to this book, a contract is a legal matter. It is strongly recommended that you consult with a lawyer as to the terms, both included and excluded, in any contract that you are about to sign.

The sample contract included in Chapter 13 – The Contractor's Toolbox should also be reviewed by your lawyer. There are terms in the sample agreement that are written primarily from the client's advantage and should perhaps be re-written to suit your particular desires. Particularly note the issues around "confidentiality" and "non-solicitation." You may have a desire to retain title to any intellectual property that you develop so that you can apply your developments to future clients. This should be expressly stated in the contract.

In 2009, when my son was contemplating operating as an independent contractor, we used the sample contract as a starting point. His payer did not have a standard agreement in place for working with contractors, despite the fact that the use of independent contractors was quite common. We made numerous changes to the draft contract before coming up with something that was satisfactory to all parties.

You may not want the non-competition terms to prevent you from seeking work with a particular company, particularly if you are contracting through a placement firm or another consulting company.

It is essential that you refer to the discussion above, which basically lays out the "elements of a good contract." The discussion sets out contract terms that serve to protect you from being considered an employee or a "personal service business/company" rather than an independent contractor. The dialogue also sets out terms that should be considered with respect to other more abstract matters.

CHAPTER 9

Cash Management

"Precious treasure remains in a wise man's dwelling;
but a foolish man devours it."

— Proverbs 21:20

While this chapter may be the shortest in the book, cash management is perhaps the most important issue for an independent contractor to become and remain successful from a financial standpoint.

Whether the issue is managing the cash on hand, looking at having ready access to funds if you are between contracts or securing your long term financial future, you need to be proactive in your approach. You should be discussing your financial position and net worth with your accountant. He can assist you to plan your finances in advance, thereby avoiding any unpleasant surprises along the way.

Pools of Cash

One of the overriding characteristics of an independent contractor's corporation is that it will build up a significant amount of cash very quickly. This is particularly true during the Corporation's first fiscal year. The first fiscal year is significant because there are no tax installments required until after the end of that fiscal year. Obviously, if the company has not made appropriate tax installments, there is going to be a significant liability for taxes at the end of the corporate year. It is therefore imperative that the independent contractor properly manage cash on hand. It is important that the cash be put to work rather than sitting in your current bank account. Otherwise, you succeed only in making your banker very happy. You must keep in mind that all of the accumulated cash really does not belong to you. It is there to meet other obligations and you must plan to have the cash available when the obligations become due.

Within your company, you require funds to finance the day to day operations. For an independent contractor, this is usually a minimal amount. These are funds that are to be held in your operating bank account and not be otherwise invested. This money will cover any day-to-day expenses as well as the funds that you need to draw from the company for your own personal expenses. Beyond this basic amount retained in your operating account, there are three pools of funds that should be invested as follows:

Pool One

The first pool is to fund the annual corporate income taxes, HST/GST, and source deductions. It will also cover remittances in provinces that assess other payroll related taxes. These tax amounts are due at specific times and may be a significant amount depending on your income level in the company and how much you are drawing in the form of salary.

This pool should be invested such that the principal is safe and liquid. You may need to access these funds on short notice and they should be worth a dollar for dollar invested on the day you need them. For this pool you should consider a high interest savings account or a money market mutual fund. With the interest rates in effect in early 2013, it may not seem worth the trouble to spend the time investing in these types of investment vehicles. Consider, however, that you may have as much as $50,000 invested on average at between 1% and 2%. The return is not very significant; however, it is still much better than leaving the funds in a non-interest-bearing account. The amount to be accumulated in this pool is determined by the level of your income.

The key is to have sufficient cash set aside in this pool to meet all your tax obligations as and when they come due. If you automatically set aside 30% of your gross income, regardless how much you gross, the pool should be sufficient to meet all your HST/GST, payroll source deductions and corporate income taxes. In most cases, at 30%, you should be getting a start on the second pool of cash.

Pool Two

The second pool is an emergency reserve fund in case you are between contracts for an extended period of time. Ideally, you would move from one contract to the next with only a short or no break depending on the length of the contracts. That is not always the case.

Being able to select the type of contract and type of work that you want to do is one of the primary non-financial advantages of independent contracting. This is a key factor in ensuring that you are enjoying the work that you are doing on a daily basis. On the other hand, an employee must do whatever his employer requires of him each day. Having a reserve pool of funds available allows you to be able to pick the next contract. Without the pool, you may be forced to accept whatever is available at the time and the work might not suit you. You may even be forced to accept a permanent position.

This pool should also be conservatively invested. You again want to ensure that the principal is safe and somewhat liquid. You may be able to select longer term investments than what you are using in the first pool of funds. This can be investment vehicles such as term deposits and bond or mortgage funds. By staggering maturities of your term deposits, you can provide for a constant cash flow for yourself if required.

How much do you need in this pool? The amount to be accumulated in this account should be between four and six months of your personal living expenses. The amount that you set aside for yourself is dependent upon what other personal funds you might have to fall back on, what the local market for contractor work is like, and how comfortable you would feel should you have to sit and wait for the right opportunity to come along.

Pool Three

The final pool is essentially funds accumulated in excess of the other requirements listed above. When you have looked after your tax and operating liabilities, you are ready to start your investment pool. With this pool you are essentially creating a pension plan for yourself within your company. This pool is a supplement to your RRSP which allows you more flexibility than the RRSP might.

This pool should be invested for long term growth. You are generally looking at investing in stocks, bonds, mutual funds and real estate according to your own risk sensitivity. You should definitely consider using a financial advisor to assist with your investments in this pool.

Your next consideration is the tax efficiency of the investments that you choose. Overall, you want to make investments that provide a good return, however you need to consider the after-tax return as well as the actual return that is received. Various types of income may be received and they may all be taxed differently according to their nature. The tax efficiency of various types of income is discussed in Chapter 11.

Caution

I caution that investment funds held inside your operating company are subject to any liability claims that may be made against your company. This can be mitigated by carrying professional liability insurance and/or creating a holding company. As the cost of operating a holding company (primarily accounting and bank fees) can be significant, you should consider following that route of protection only once a certain (unspecified) level of investments have been accumulated. The level of investment needed and the timing to pursue this approach will depend not only on the cost/benefit of doing it, but on your own degree of risk aversion.

CHAPTER 10

Owner Remuneration - How Do I Pay Myself?

Accessing Corporate Funds

How do I get the money out of my corporation?

This is perhaps the question we hear asked most often by the new independent contractor and very often by those who have been operating their own corporation for several years. The answer is, "It depends." As a shareholder/director of your company you have some options as to how you get money out of your company. Which option is best for you is determined by a number of factors, some of which are in conflict with other factors. The determination of the ideal option for you is part science and part art.

The Options

The shareholder/director has several options for accessing the funds in his/her corporation:

<u>Temporary Measures:</u>

Drawings: At least on a temporary basis the independent contractor may simply draw funds from the company as they are required to meet personal and living expenses and possibly to pay company expenses on behalf of the company. We call these drawings, "directors' advances against expenses." These drawings must be "repaid" on a timely basis or they are to be considered as taxable employment income in the hands of the shareholder/director while the company is not allowed a tax deduction. There is provision for the taxpayer to get a credit for any subsequent repayment of the drawings, however in the meantime you and your company are subject to a form of double taxation.

Funds drawn in the current fiscal year are normally to be repaid by the end of the next fiscal year in order to avoid the income inclusion as noted above. There are several ways to "repay" these drawings. "Drawings" are not a form of remuneration. Canada Revenue Agency will sometimes try to consider the drawings as a salary to you, however the repayment may be in the form of an actual repayment from personal funds by either you or your spouse, the payment of a salary (director's fee) to you or to your spouse where you leave the net after source deductions in the company to offset the amounts drawn, the declaration of a dividend to either you or your spouse where again the funds are not drawn out of the company or it can be considered a loan to you in your capacity as an employee under certain specific circumstances. The repayment could be any combination of the above options.

In the majority of cases, our clients only take drawings throughout the fiscal year as they require funds. At the end of the company's fiscal year we assess how much the directors have drawn and set a salary and/or dividend to "repay "the drawings.

The drawings are not generally subject to any interest charge as they are advances to an employee to cover possible expenses incurred on behalf of the company. Such advances are to be repaid to the company as at the fiscal year end of the company. If not repaid as at that date, there is an interest charge to be reported as a taxable benefit on the directors T4 slip for that fiscal year. This benefit is a deemed interest charge at the "prescribed rate" as set by the government each calendar quarter. The rate is applied to the outstanding drawings until they are repaid.

Loans: As noted above, the shareholder/director can "borrow" funds from the company on a short term temporary basis with no formal agreement being set up. Technically speaking, a shareholder is not permitted to "borrow" from the company but there are three specific instances where an employee can borrow funds for a period that exceeds the end of the following fiscal year. A formal loan agreement should be drawn up to specify that the loan is made in your capacity as an employee. You should ensure that your remuneration package includes a salary component for the duration of the loan.

An employee, subject to certain conditions, can borrow to:
1. Purchase a vehicle to be used in the business,
2. Purchase a house to be used as the principal residence of the employee, and
3. Purchase additional shares of the company

These conditions include the fact that bona fide repayment terms must be in place before the loan is advanced, the loans are available to all employees on the same or similar terms and conditions and that the terms are reasonable and similar to loans advanced to employees of other corporations. There should be an audit trail to show that the withdrawn funds were used to acquire the vehicle or the house.

This is again a temporary way of getting funds out of the company. The loans must be repaid. A car loan is typically to be repaid ($1/5^{th}$ per year) over a five year term. A housing loan is repayable over a five year term ($1/10^{th}$ per year) with an option to extend it for a further five years. It should also be clear that the loans are for acquiring the asset and not for re-financing.

<u>Permanent Measures:</u>

Salary (Directors fees): A salary is one of the forms of remuneration and represents a permanent way of removing funds from the company. Most of our clients are familiar with salaries as they have generally had some form of employment before becoming an independent contractor. Even with that experience, how the Canada Pension contributions and Income Taxes are withheld and remitted to the Government are foreign concepts to most new contractors.

The payment of a salary requires the company to withhold Canada Pension contributions and income tax from the payment to the employee. The company is then required to remit (pay) those amounts to the government on a time sensitive basis. The company also has to match the Canada Pension Plan contribution when making that remittance.

The salary is a deduction for the company together with the company portion of Canada Pension. The salary is essentially a means to transfer income from the corporate tax system to the individual tax system. The company gets the deduction for the payment of the salary while the employee is taxed for the remuneration received. As such there is no double taxation with the payment of a salary by the corporation to the director (employee) of the company.

Consulting/Management Fees: On rare occasions, a contractor may "sub-contract" or provide services to his corporation on a personal basis. He invoices the company for his services and if the fees charged exceed $30,000 he must be registered and charge the company GST on those fees. The fees are a deduction for the company, as is a salary, and they are taxable in the personal tax return of the consultant.

We don't normally recommend this form of remuneration for several reasons:

1. First, Canada Revenue Agency simply does not like this approach and using it may increase the likelihood of an audit.
2. Second, as it is impossible to get around "controlling" yourself, it is unlikely that you meet the criteria to be an independent contractor to your own company, thereby opening the door to being considered an employee. If considered an employee, the company may become subject to penalty and interest for failing to withhold payroll source deductions and

remitting them on a timely basis.

3. Finally, there is yet another set of GST returns to be prepared and filed. You do need to be careful what method you are using to calculate your GST. You don't want to be charging your company GST if it is using the "Quick Method" to determine its liability to the government.

Except if you are late for remitting source deductions, there is little advantage in fees versus a salary. You will still be subject to paying Canada Pension contributions on your personal tax return and will have to charge GST if you are charging in excess of $30,000. Once registered for GST you will have to charge the tax even if the fees are less than the threshold amount in a subsequent year.

Dividends: A dividend is the other method of permanently removing funds from the company. The dividend is essentially a return on the investment you made in your company through the purchase of shares. It is not technically a form of remuneration although we often consider it an alternative way of remunerating the owner-manager. Unlike the salary, the dividend is not a deduction for the company in determining the corporate income. The dividend is paid from the company's retained earnings. Retained earnings are funds that are left after the corporate taxes have been computed and paid.

There are several types of dividends and how they are taxed differs by their nature.

Ordinary dividends are the most common for the independent contractor and small businesses where the net annual earnings are below $400,000. A dividend allows income to be taxed at the corporate level and at the individual level. The Canadian tax systems are designed to eliminate this double taxation through an integration process. As the dividend is paid from the company's after tax income we use a gross-up and tax credit process to eliminate the double taxation that would otherwise result. Prior to the 2013 federal budget, a dividend of $100 will be reported in your personal tax return as $125 of taxable income. You will then receive a tax credit in the tax calculation of 13.33% of the grossed up amount. The 2013 federal budget is proposing changes to the gross up and tax credit rates which will provide a closer integration between the taxes paid on a salary and on a dividend. This will result in higher taxes being paid on dividends than has previously been the case. This makes it all the more important for you to discuss the salary/ dividend issue with your accountant before the source deductions for a salary are due.

Special Dividends:

Capital Dividends are amounts declared paid from a notional tax account that tracks the cumulative net capital gains/losses that the company has earned. The tracking starts with the incorporation of your company. Your company is taxed on only half of the capital gains it earns and is allowed to apply only one half of any capital losses. The untaxed half is tracked in the notional tax account called the "Capital Dividend Account" (CDA). This net untaxed portion of the capital gain retains its nature and at some point you can file an election to have a dividend paid from this account. That dividend is tax free to you. The balance of the CDA must be properly computed and an election form must be submitted to Canada Revenue Agency on a timely basis together with a special directors' resolution.

Eligible Dividends are dividends where the company has paid tax at the general tax rates. As these rates are much higher than the small business rates, the dividend gross-up and tax credit are much greater than with ordinary dividends. Income taxed at the general tax rates and investment income in the form of eligible dividends is tracked in another notional tax account called the "General Rate Income Pool" (GRIP). The company at some time may declare a dividend to be paid from the GRIP allowing you as an a shareholder to benefit from the higher gross-up and tax credit.

★ ★ ★ ★ ★

The Salary/Dividend Decision

One of the basic issues for independent contractors and most business owner-managers is whether a salary (director's fee) or a dividend is the optimal method to extract funds from the company. The optimal decision for one individual may not be the best solution for another. This is a very personal decision. Although your accountant will normally make the decision on your behalf in many cases, he/she generally needs some good input as to your preferences. In many cases a combination of a salary and a dividend is used. Depending on the province you are in, the tax advantage/disadvantage of salary or dividend will vary in accordance with provincial tax and credit levels. With the changes in the 2013 federal budget, the advantage of a dividend in your province may be eliminated. It may actually become a penalty, so it is important to do some forward planning with respect to the salary dividend determination.

As part of the determination there are three things you must determine:

1. The amount to be paid. I always encouraged our clients to retain funds inside their corporation for various reasons, so the objective is to try to limit the amount to be paid out as either a salary or a dividend. Generally we limit the remuneration to the amount required to cover your net drawings for the year although maximizing the use of the low tax brackets is often factored in.

2. The allocation of the remuneration. In the setup of your company you should have probably considered including your spouse (and in rare occasions your children) as shareholders and/or directors. The purpose in doing this is to enable you to sprinkle the income to you and your spouse to allow more income to be taxed in lower tax brackets.

3. Whether the remuneration is to be by way of salary, dividend or some combination.

The discussion below is primarily related to situations where the small business deduction is applicable for the corporation. The considerations below are the ones primarily encountered and may not reflect all options.

Factors that Favour Dividends:

- At least until the 2013 federal budget takes effect, in most provinces, remuneration by way of all dividends generally results in the lowest overall combined corporate and personal taxes. The assumed point at which integration between the corporate and personal systems is when the corporate tax rate is about 20%. In most provinces the rate is below 20% and results in over-integration. The result is a slight bias towards dividends.
- Timing. Clients that tend to file late may be better off to pay only dividends. The remittance of source deductions for a salary and filing of late T4 (salary) and T5 (dividend) returns are events that attract significant penalties. The late filer is often better off to reflect only dividends rather than incur the penalties for late remittances on a salary.
- Refundable Dividend Tax on Hand. A company pays taxes on investment income that are potentially refundable. Your corporation recovers this tax by paying taxable dividends to its shareholders. This can reduce the overall tax rate for the corporation.
- Cash flow considerations. The payment of a salary requires the company to withhold Canada Pension and Income tax from the owner-manager's wages. The company must remit these amounts and match the Canada Pension contributions on a time sensitive basis to avoid penalties. No withholdings and remittances are required for dividends. The taxes are paid

on filing your personal tax return in April. (Even where the tax may be slightly higher with dividends than with a salary, the cash outflow may be less as no CPP premiums need to be paid.)

- Canada Pension benefits are maximized. Currently, in determining CPP benefits reference is made to your contributions over your working life. The lowest 15% of years are dropped from the calculation. A contractor should be encouraged to get the CPP report from the government to indicate their CPP entitlement. It is possible that further contributions may not improve the benefit amount you will receive.

- Ontario contractors are subject to the Ontario Employee Health Tax on salaries paid. Dividends are not subject to this tax.

Factors That Favour Salaries (Director Fees):

- In some provinces there is an advantage to salary over dividends due to the corporate tax rate exceeding the integration level or particularly low personal tax rates

- A salary allows you to make contributions to Canada Pension. The amount that you contribute will affect your ultimate pension from the plan. No contributions are applicable with dividends. With today's maximum contribution well over $2,000 and to be matched by the company, the owner-manager may view CPP as an expense rather than a benefit.

- A salary builds contribution room for Registered Retirement Savings Plan (RRSP) contributions. Dividends are not "earned income" and do not create RRSP room.

- If you have borrowed funds from your company "in your capacity as an employee" to acquire a vehicle to be used in the business or to assist you in obtaining your principal residence, then you need to take some portion of your remuneration in the form of a salary. This might also be the case if you are insured under some personal health care plans (review your obligations for the plan).

- A salary reduces corporate income and therefore corporate taxes. This translates to lower the requirement for corporate tax instalments. On the other hand a dividend does not reduce corporate taxes and likely increases the owner-manager's requirement to pay personal tax instalments.
- Tax deferral can be achieved with a bonus salary. A salary can be accrued in the financial statements to reduce corporate tax. The actual payment of that bonus can be deferred for 179 days from the fiscal year end. The source deductions would then be due the following month.
- Insurance (particularly disability insurance, including WCB coverage) and other benefits may be tied to the level of salary. Disability plans are often wage replacement plans. If there has been no wage the insurance company may limit or forego the payment of benefits.
- As there is no gross-up of income with a salary, the payment of salary to a senior rather than a dividend may be less likely to cause a claw-back of Old Age Security or reduction of the Age Amount.
- Some deductions, such as child care, are based on earned income and may require the payment of a salary to be able to make a claim or to have the deduction claimed by the appropriate spouse.
- Any self-employed individual who has tried to secure a mortgage through conventional lending organizations will know it is difficult unless you have a significant salary. Bankers do not seem to comprehend that a dividend is just as valid a remuneration as a salary. They do not seem to give a dividend any weight in determining your capacity for a mortgage and tend to rely not only on you having a salary but also the amount of it. If you are planning the purchase of a house, you may need to take remuneration by way of a salary and possibly in amounts greater than would normally be prudent in order to

qualify for your mortgage.

- A spouse that has a job outside of the corporation will be paying Employment Insurance premiums on that income. They cannot opt out of the coverage. If this spouse takes time off for maternity leave, you need to be concerned with your income limits with Employment Insurance. EI auditors will try to include not only dividends received from your company, but may also try to attribute the company net income (not dividends or salary) to the individual in an attempt to exclude you from benefits that you have paid premiums to be covered for. Dividends are not employment income and a shareholder does not have any specific right to the income earned by a company. Back in chapter 6 we learned that a corporation is a separate legal entity, so a shareholder has no means to enforce receiving income from that corporation. During a maternity leave, a spouse should not draw either a salary or a dividend to provide you with a strong argument to exclude company income from that considered as your income. The attempts by EI (and the courts) to include dividends and company net income as your income for EI purposes is contradictory to other legislation and in my opinion is simply dishonest.

CHAPTER 11

Investment Philosophy

In Chapter 9, we discussed how important it was for the independent contractor to properly manage his cash flow and the funds retained in his corporation. In that chapter, we looked at the three major pools of funds that the consultant should be considering. It should be pointed out that all three of these pools of funds are to remain in the Corporation until required by the contractor. The first cash pool is required to meet outside liabilities. These liabilities include both commercial liabilities and corporate tax liabilities. The second pool is intended to cover ongoing commercial liabilities, but it is primarily to ensure that the independent contractor has funds available for personal needs if he is between contracts for an extended period of time.

The third pool of money, is intended to be invested for long term growth. This pool of money is looked at as the contractors pension plan. While the funds remaining in the Corporation are to be put to work for you, they should be invested in a tax efficient manner. Different types of income are taxed at different rates and in different ways according to their nature. This may require the assistance of a professional investment advisor. There are, however certain types of investments that generate kinds of income that are taxed more efficiently in your Corporation than other kinds of income.

In this chapter we are going to look at a couple of the most common types of registered plans for investment and we will also look at the kinds of income that are taxed more efficiently in your Corporation.

Registered Retirement Savings Plan (RRSP)

A Registered Retirement Savings Plan is a scheme whereby the taxpayer is able to make an annual contribution, within limits, and be allowed to deduct that contribution on his personal income tax return. The plan must be registered with the government in order to allow you to make this deduction. The RRSP is perhaps the greatest tax deferral tool that is available to most Canadian tax payers. The registered retirement savings plan is not an investment vehicle in and of itself as the particular investments held within the RRSP can cover a vast range of investments and investment types. Essentially, the RRSP is a means to defer tax by allowing you to deduct your annual contribution to be taxed along with the income that it earns, when you withdraw the funds from the RRSP.

Registered Retirement Savings Plans were initially intended as a means for the ordinary taxpayer to set aside funds for their retirement. Unless you work for the government or a major corporation, it is unlikely that you will have access to a pension plan when you retire. The RRSP was instituted for those taxpayers who are not otherwise taken care of. You are permitted to contribute to an RRSP, based on your "contribution room." Contribution room is calculated with respect to your "earned income" according to your personal tax return. If you make contributions to a registered pension plan, your ability to contribute to an RRSP may be restricted. Excess contributions will result in a penalty tax.

You should note that an RRSP is a personal plan. Your corporation cannot make a contribution to an RRSP and receive a deduction for that contribution. Your company can make the payment to an RRSP on your behalf, however that contribution will be included as part of your personal income.

In recent years, the federal government has provided legislation that will enable you to use your RRSP for alternative projects without having to take the withdrawal as personal income. Primary in these alternatives is the home buyers plan. This plan allows a first-time homebuyer, to withdraw a certain amount that can be applied as a down payment toward their purchase. This amount must be repaid over a 15 year time period. If the taxpayer fails to make the required annual repayment, the amount of that repayment is included in the taxpayer's income for the year.

The government has also enacted legislation to allow you to use your RRSP to help finance your education. They have created what is known as a lifelong learning plan, which allows you to withdraw funds for the purpose of funding your education. Again the withdrawal must be repaid over a specified time frame; other-wise the required repayment amount will be included in income for that year.

You can withdraw funds at any time from your RRSP. If the withdrawal is not used for one of the designated purposes, the withdrawal is taxed in your personal tax return.

Your RRSP can become a future income splitting technique. The government will allow you to contribute to what is known as a spousal RRSP, in which case you still get a tax deduction on your return, however your contribution goes into a plan for your spouse. At some point in the future, your spouse may withdraw funds from the spousal plan and the withdrawal will be taxed in their hands, rather than in your hands. How it works is that you, likely with a high income, get the deduction and your spouse, likely in a low tax bracket claims the income.

First, I do recommend that you contribute to an RRSP. However, RRSPs are not the be all and end all and they do have some disadvantages that are seldom discussed. I also recommend that you use excess funds in your company for investment purposes (within the company) as well.

You can withdraw funds from the company and invest them outside the company and outside an RRSP, however to get the money out of the company you have to take taxable income. This leaves you with perhaps only 64 or 68 cents on the dollar to invest. As the company pays a very low rate of tax, you are left with 86 cents (Alberta) on the dollar to be invested within the company. For this reason, it is best to leave funds in the company and invest them there rather than to withdraw them.

When we talked about the third pool of cash, we looked to have you invest for long term growth. Essentially what we're looking at is wealth creation. Wealth is financial independence, it is not income. It is the assets that you have accumulated and can draw on for future income. A typical independent contractor is a high income earner. It is this characteristic that allows him to accumulate financial assets in a short period of time. It really doesn't matter how much you earn today, it is your ability to set aside funds for the future that determines your true wealth.

We encourage you to begin earning and investing early in your adult life. The RRSP is the tax advantaged plan that will assist you in accumulating funds for the future. Let's have a look at what contributing early will do for you:

Accumulation — early contribution

If starting at age 20 you contribute $2000 per year for 10 years and then stop contributing, you would make a total contribution of $20,000. If you are to earn interest at the rate of 6% on your contributions, the value of your RRSP at age 65 would be $202,621.

Accumulation – midlife contribution

If you waited instead until age 35, at which point you contribute $5000 per year for 10 years, you would make a total contribution of $50,000. If you are to earn interest at the rate of 6% on your contributions; the value of your RRSP at age 65 would be $211,363. You have contributed $30,000 more than if you started 15 years earlier and you have increased the value of your RRSP by less than $10,000.

Accumulation – late contribution

If you did not begin your contributions until age 50, and at that point you contributed $12,000 a year for 10 years, you would make a total contribution of $120,000. Again, if the interest rate remains unchanged at 6% to age 65, value of your RRSP at that time will accumulate to $211,667. In postponing your contributions to later in life, you will have to contribute significantly more to accumulate approximately the same amount on retirement.

Obviously, it does pay to begin your savings at an early age. It would also be beneficial to continue making contributions through your working life, rather than for a limited number of years as used in the examples above.

There is a day of reckoning for your RRSP. An RRSP is taxed:
- on withdrawal,
- when a special plan is not repaid, and/or
- on death. [Unless rolled over to a spouse or dependent child].

The tax deferral afforded by an RRSP becomes somewhat limited after you have attained the age of 71. At this point, you must convert your RRSP into a registered retirement income fund (RRIF), which requires you to withdraw and pay tax on a graduated portion of your accumulated funds on an annual basis.

Tax-Free Savings Account (TFSA)

A recent addition to a registered account is what is known as the tax-free savings account. The TFSA, is a system whereby you can contribute up to $5000 a year and the savings account will earn income that is tax-free. The contribution to the savings account does not generate a tax deduction, as does an RRSP contribution. It is the income earned within the plan that becomes sheltered and is not included on your personal tax return. The TFSA does not have any restrictions on how you can use the funds. The withdrawals from the TFSA are not taxed when you take the money out. You received no deduction when you made your contribution and you pay no tax when the money comes out. The income earned within the plan is never taxed.

Tax-free savings account is of value when you have funds that are not in a registered plan and are held outside your Corporation and are earning income for you. You should move these funds into a tax-free savings account to shelter the funds from tax on the income earned.

I have had clients indicate that they would like to withdraw funds from the Corporation to put into a tax-free savings account. This is really not a viable action to take, as they will have to pay tax on the money they withdraw from the company, leaving them with perhaps $.65 on the dollar to put into the tax-free savings account.

★ ★ ★ ★ ★

Leaving funds in Your Corporation.

The RRSP and the TFSA are investment plans for an individual. When we're looking at the third pool of cash that has accumulated in your company, we are thinking more along the lines of leaving that cash in the company. We certainly don't want it left as cash sitting in the current account because that will not provide a return for you. You need to get the money working for you. This third pool of cash can be considered to be funds that you are setting aside as a pension fund, so you want to have the money invested for long term growth. In Chapter 9 we discussed the first two pools of money and indicated that those funds needed to be invested in liquid or relatively liquid investments and the investment should also be fairly conservative. When those funds are needed, you want them to be worth at least a dollar for dollar invested.

Ideally, you will not need to draw on the funds that comprise the third pool of cash. It is therefore possible to invest in longer-term investments such as capital stock, government and corporate bonds, mutual funds and perhaps, real estate.

I caution that investment funds held inside your operating company are subject to any liability claims that may be made against your company. This can be mitigated by carrying professional liability insurance and/or creating a holding company. As the cost of operating a holding company (primarily accounting and bank fees) can be significant, you will want to consider this option of asset protection only once a certain (unspecified) level of investments have been accumulated. Keep in mind that Errors and Omissions insurance is not inexpensive either.

With a potential claw back of Old Age Security pension funds should your income exceed a base level, having funds in your company rather than outside it allows you to manage the annual flow of personal income to you. This may not eliminate a claw back entirely, but you may be able to alternate high and low income years in order to keep you below the threshold in alternate years.

Investing in Real Estate

When I was considering what I might write in this section of the book, I looked back at a seminar I had given to my Associates in "CA4IT" several years ago. My notes indicate that I started that seminar indicating that our clients had a lack of confidence in the current state of the stock market. I think that angst is still present today and is combined with what are record low interest rates, at least within my lifetime. It is extremely difficult to motivate someone to move money from a current account even to a long-term investment that will provide perhaps a 1% to 1 1/4% return on the investment.

The bleak outlook for investment with respect to interest rates and the performance of the stock market led many contractors to consider investing their excess funds in real estate. Once they had decided that this would provide them with the best return, the next question to resolve was whether or not it is better to invest personally (personal funds) or to purchase the property within their corporation (corporate cash). Fact is that there are pros and cons making that investment either personally or within the company.

Individual Ownership

One of the overall advantages of investing in real estate, whether the property is owned individually or by the company, is that you can generally leverage your investment in using a small down payment and borrowing the balance for your investment. When you rent out or lease the property, your tenant will help to repay the financing through the rent they pay.

One of the overall disadvantages of investing in real estate, whether the property is owned individually or by the company, is that you may have tenants that failed to pay their rent and/or disappear on you in the middle of the night. You may have tenants that may have no respect for your property and do a considerable amount of damage, which you cannot recover from them. You will also have ongoing repairs and maintenance, which will require your time, should you be lucky enough to have the skills to make those repairs yourself. Otherwise you will have to hire repairmen at their going rate.

The positive items of individual ownership start with your ability to claim depreciation (capital cost allowance in tax terms) as an expense during the year. The depreciation is based on the cost of the building and any chattels. The cost of building and chattels are paid for by your down payment and the financing that you received. This means that you pay these costs as and when you repay the mortgage. The depreciation expense does not agree to any cash flow. So it helps you reduce your taxable income and possibly create a positive cash flow. A positive cash flow may be used for other personal purposes.

Rental income is considered as passive income, and therefore is not eligible for the small business tax rate. In many of the provinces therefore, once refundable taxes are paid by a corporation on passive income, the corporate tax rate may be higher than what you are looking at on a personal basis. The difference may be negligible. If your company pays a taxable dividend it recovers the refundable portion of corporate tax making the corporate rate comparable with the top personal rates. It is quite typical however, for a rental property to have losses in the first few years that the property is owned. This generally is a result of paying interest on a substantial amount of mortgage. These losses can be applied against other personal income which might be from employment or other investments. This reduces your tax on this other income and provides a better cash flow to you.

If you're looking to finance a significant portion of the investment, you should consider that an individual may be able to mortgage a rental property with 75% to 90% of the purchase price financed. A Corporation will likely be restricted to a maximum of about 60% of the market value of the rental property for financing.

On the downside for owning rental property personally, funds are generally only available from the Corporation. This will require you to declare additional salary and/or dividend and could push your individual income to a higher tax bracket. Any down payment or financing of ongoing losses are required to be paid by the individual owner. In order to meet these cash flow demands, the individual will continue to have to draw additional funds from the corporation. With the additional draws, there might be only $.65 on the dollar left after taxes to cover the cash flow requirements.

Corporate Ownership

Among the advantages of corporate ownership is the fact that you are using a limited liability company. This benefit should be taken with a grain of salt as I refer you back to chapter 6, where we looked at the characteristics of each of the forms of organization. The ability of the creditor to go after any of your personal assets, unless of course you've given a personal guarantee, may be limited by the shelter that the corporation provides you.

As we noted earlier, your rental property may result in some ongoing cash deficiencies, particularly in the early years of ownership. Active business income generated within your company, which is taxed at the low rate, could be used for the purchase and finance of these ongoing cash deficiencies as required.

With respect to estate planning matters, it may be easier to transfer the shares of the company, administer the property within the company including the payment of dividends to the estate beneficiaries, than through numerous individual undivided ownership interests of beneficiaries with an individually owned rental property or properties.

Downside of corporate ownership starts with the fact that any positive net taxable income is taxed as investment income of the top corporate rates. When refundable dividend tax is factored in on this passive income, the overall corporate tax rate will likely be higher than the top personal tax rates. This means that more tax will be paid on rental income through corporate ownership than if the property was held personally. This higher tax rate can be mitigated if the Corporation were to pay taxable dividends to its shareholders and thereby recover a portion of the refundable dividend tax.

Qualified small business corporations qualify for a potential enhanced capital gain exemption with respect to its otherwise active business being carried on. Investments held within the company, whether they be real estate or other investments, may disqualify a corporation from being considered a "Qualified Small Business Corporation" for purposes of this capital gain exemption. The capital gain exemption comes into play, when a shareholder decides to sell his shares of the small business corporation. The capital stock of a consulting company operating as an independent contractor would rarely be sold to a third-party. The only time that the sale of the shares would become relevant, is on the death of the shareholder.

There is a possibility of double taxation arising on death due to the deemed disposition of the shareholder shares at fair market value (which is determined by taking into account the market value of the real estate owned by the company), and then having the same real estate value being taxed again when it is ultimately sold by the company and distributed as dividends to the beneficiary share-holders. One way of avoiding this problem would be to have the company wind up within one year of death. Another, perhaps more practical way to avoid the problem, is to have the shares transferred to a spouse on death thereby deferring the tax on the value of the shares up to the date of the spouse's demise. In the interim period, the investment properties can be liquidated and perhaps paid out in a more tax efficient manner.

Rather than paying additional salary and/or dividends to a shareholder to finance the purchase of a rental property and cover operating deficiencies, a Corporation could make a tax-free loan to assist your company or other related Corporation for real estate investment purposes. While this procedure may avoid the tax drain on these funds, you do need to be concerned about losses incurred in a separate company. If the real estate is owned in a separate company and is incurring losses, those losses may be trapped in that company and not be usable against other income of the shareholder or the operating company.

Conclusion

It will be necessary for you to assess all these pros and cons as they apply to your personal situation before making a real estate investment. Over the years, my conclusion has been that if you have the funds outside of your company, then you should make the investment personally. It really doesn't make sense to invest personal funds into your company, and purchase the real estate inside the company.

In most cases, the funds will be sourced inside the company. Generally speaking in such cases the real estate investment should be made inside the Corporation or in a related company. As noted earlier, it may be easier to obtain a greater portion of the purchase price through financing if the investment is made on an individual basis. This means that you need to consider the overall level of the investment required to determine where the ownership should lie.

When you are considering making the investment, one thing to keep in mind is that the ownership of assets can only be transferred out of the company at their fair market value. Whereas an asset originally owned by an individual, could usually be rolled tax-free into a corporation if the circumstances warranted a change.

Tax Efficient Investing

Your next consideration is the tax efficiency of the investments that you choose. First and foremost, you want to make investments that provide a good return, however you need to consider the after-tax return as well as the actual return that is received. Various types of income may be received and they may all be taxed differently according to their nature.

For those not familiar with the concept of dividends, it is strongly recommended that you discuss the issues with both your accountant and a reliable investment advisor. Your advisor may want to discuss your specific situation with your accountant as well.

Refundable Dividend Tax

Investment income, including real estate income, is a passive type of income and is not eligible for the small business deduction. Investment income (other than dividends) is generally taxed at the general rates applicable depending on which province the company is based in. Most dividends are excluded from income tax, but are taxed under Part IV of the Income Tax Act. A portion of the Part I tax (income tax) and the Part IV tax are potentially refundable to your company. These refundable taxes are assessed as an incentive to have you pay dividends and remove the income from your company rather than parking the income inside the corporation. These taxes form what is called the Refundable Dividend Tax. This tax can be recovered at a rate of $1 for every $3 of taxable dividends that your company pays. As long as the company has paid this refundable tax, that tax can be recovered through the payment of a taxable dividend. If you pay a $300 dividend, you will receive a $100 refund or more appropriately a credit against the current year taxes. You can pay a higher dividend, but you only receive a credit to the extent that you have refundable tax accumulated.

I mentioned tax-efficiency in looking at the after-tax return you might receive. When you make an investment, you should consider more than the actual return it will provide to you. While certain types of investment income are taxed more efficiently in your company than other types, a 14% return on a tax inefficient investment is still better than a 4% return on something that is more lightly taxed. On the other hand, most returns are closer than those figures and an investment in an asset that provides tax efficient income will likely result in a better after-tax return.

Interest income is not taxed in an efficient manner. Although I have suggested investments for the first two pools of cash in chapter 9 that provide interest income, I do so for reasons other than getting you the best after-tax return. The overriding criterion for those pools is safety of principal and liquidity. It is in the pension pool that you should be considering tax efficiency. The types of income that are taxed more efficiently would be capital gains, public company dividends and return of capital. Actually, return of capital is not income. It is a return of your principal and reduces the cost base of your investment while providing you with a cash flow.

Capital Gains

Only 50% of capital gains are taxable. On a $100 gain, your company pays tax at the general investment rate. The 50% that is not taxed is tracked in a notional tax account called the Capital Dividend Account along with the net capital losses. If you have a positive balance in this account, at some point you can file an election to declare a dividend to be paid from this notional tax account. That is called a Capital Dividend and it comes out of the company to you tax free. A capital gain earned in an RRSP, on the other hand, eventually is paid as pension income and is taxed on 100% of the gain. In this case it would be better to earn a capital gain inside your company than in a registered retirement savings plan.

Public Company Dividends:

Generally dividends from Canadian Public companies are deductible in determining taxable income for your company. They are then taxed under Part IV of the Income Tax Act and you pay a "refundable tax" of 1/3 of the dividend. As noted above, the company can recover this tax when it pays a taxable dividend at the rate of $1 of tax for every $3 of dividend paid.

When you pay a dividend from your company, there is a gross up and tax credit process to integrate the personal tax system and the corporate tax system to eliminate double taxation. Until a few years ago, this relief did not exist for public company dividends. Now, dividends paid to an individual go through a gross up and tax credit process as well. For example; using 2012 Saskatchewan tax rates, you can pay a dividend from your company which has had the benefit of the small business deduction. Assuming you had no other income, you could pay and receive personally a dividend of $20,000 and have very minimal tax (~ $100) to pay personally. If your only income was an "eligible" dividend from a public company, you could receive as much as $48,000 before you would start to pay any personal taxes.

The public company pays taxes at the higher general tax rates and as such the gross up and tax credit are much higher than those from your own company which pays taxes at the lower small business rate. When your company receives a dividend from a public company, the dividend is tracked in another notional tax account called the "General Rate Income Pool" (GRIP). At some point you may elect to pay a dividend from this pool and that dividend will retain the same nature and provide the "eligible" gross up and tax credit being effectively taxed at a much lower rate in your hands than other income would be.

Return of Capital:

Some investments will provide you with a cash flow or re-investment that is characterized as a return of capital. It is effectively returning a small portion of your investment to you. This is not considered as taxable income, so the company does not pay tax on it. The receipt does reduce the carrying value of your investment. If the investment retains the funds, it will be re-invested for you increasing the shares/units that you hold. If it actually cashes out to you, you can take the funds and reinvest them elsewhere. Down the road when you sell the investment, even if it is for less than you originally paid, you are likely to realize a capital gain on the disposal as you are comparing your proceeds to the reduced cost base. This again puts you back in the situation discussed above where there is a benefit to receiving capital gains.

Investments in stocks will provide the dividend and potentially capital gain income while mutual funds may provide all three of the above types of income/cash flow and more. I had the opportunity to meet with some of the executives of "NexGen Financial" which has a family of mutual funds which will allow you to specify the type of income that will be allocated to you regardless of which fund(s) you have your money invested in. It is my understanding there are now other investments that will allow you the same strategy. You should ask your investment advisor about these options before you commit your funds. I met with several advisors to discuss the tax efficient investing as laid out above. Very few of them had considered these options before we met.

Conclusion

I hope that the discussions regarding the management of your funds brings you the realization that properly handling the investment of your money is a key to you moving beyond the self-employment stage to earning substantial passive income. Without properly managing your cash and company investments, the financial advantage of contracting can still elude you. It is this step that will bring you to your own financial freedom and really put you in a position to "take ownership of your career!"

CHAPTER 12

Wrap Up

"Everyone who got where he is has had to begin where he was."

– Robert Louis Stevenson

To provide a summary of what has been discussed in the book, perhaps we should look at where we started and where we end up. Independent contracting has essentially been in existence in Canada for approximately 60 years. Its origins go back to when Ralph Sazio decided to provide his coaching and management services to the Hamilton Tiger Cats Football Club through a corporation rather than as an employee. Mr. Sazio took the step primarily to seek the tax benefits of being incorporated. Naturally, the government took great exception to Mr. Sazio's entrepreneurship and brought in legislation that would essentially circumvent anyone providing their personal services through a corporate structure. This legislation is commonly known as the personal service business rules. It wasn't until the mid-eighties that the criteria for independent contracting were established by the "Wiebe Door" case.

Although Mr. Sazio's motivation was tax oriented, we discovered back in chapter 1 that people have different characteristics. Certain characteristics make for a good employee, while other characteristics make an individual more suited to being self-employed. Over the last half-century, Canada's economy has changed significantly to that of a much more service oriented nature. As a result, while many people still look to be self-employed, they are more likely to pursue an activity that is related to providing their time and knowledge than to provide a retail or manufacturing product. This has led to more individuals considering operating as an independent contractor. Unfortunately, the government mindset has not grown with the economy. As a result, there seems to be a continued reluctance to allow people to operate as independent contractors.

In today's economy the desire to operate as an independent contractor is still motivated to some degree by the tax and cash flow advantage that is available to a successful contractor. Just as I have always emphasized the financial advantage of contracting, Canada Revenue Agency has concentrated on preventing individuals from realizing the related tax benefits. Independent contracting, however, is not all about the tax and cash flow advantages. In chapter 3 we discussed a number of the non-financial advantages of independent contracting. These advantages are what my clients would emphasize to me as the reason that they are following the independent contracting opportunity. One of the key factors in today's economy is that the use of independent contractors benefits the employers who hire individuals or least their corporations as independent contractors. It is often a mutual decision to develop an independent contractor relationship rather than an employment relationship. While I firmly believe that most organizations do require a core of employees for continuity, the employment of independent contractors will make the company more efficient and certainly more competitive, both locally and internationally.

If you have determined that you would like to be an independent contractor, you need to assess your current skill set to determine if it is adequate to allow you to be successful. You may find that you need additional experience and/or some technical upgrading. If you start with a solid education and some meaningful work experience, you are likely well positioned to begin work as an independent contractor. The key to independent contracting, of course, is to secure a contract followed by consistent renewals or alternative opportunities. To ensure a steady flow of work, it is essential for you to form a network of your peers and those who may be influential in pointing you to new contracts.

Although I am aware that there are some advisors in Canada that would urge you to conduct your work as a sole proprietor, rather than through a corporation, that would seldom be my primary advice. There are definitely some situations in which operating as a sole proprietor is the appropriate course, however for the majority of those seeking to work in this format, incorporation is the only way to go. We have seen that there is a substantial financial advantage to being incorporated over operating as a sole proprietor. In the IT sector, if you are not incorporated, you are likely cutting out over 90% of your potential market.

One of the factors that lead to the financial advantage of independent contracting is the ability to claim expenses pretax as an independent contractor. Over the years, I had numerous clients come in and say that, "with my tiny little business, I don't have much in the way of expenses." I'm sure that in some cases, this was her way of saying don't charge me too much for your accounting services. In most cases, however, it was more likely that the individual had not considered the opportunity to deduct a wide range of expenses as they relate to the earning of the income. In chapter 7, we looked at the major types of expenses that should be considered by an independent contractor. The listing is not all-inclusive, nor does it suggest that everyone would have each of the expenses indicated. The expenses discussed do constitute the most common expenses that will be incurred.

Although I have painted a glowing picture of independent contracting, I would be remiss if I didn't point out that there are also a number of risks. It is in fact these risks that suggest that Canada

Revenue Agency should be more lenient than they have been in considering whether an individual is an independent contractor versus a personal service business. There are certain risks that don't show up in the contract or even in the working relationship. It is hoped that with the continuing growth of independent contracting, the government will take a more realistic view of the nature of the business being operated. The courts have already indicated that the intention of the parties involved is the primary criteria to be considered. Should that happen, the personal service business rules would effectively become obsolete. In the meantime, it is incumbent upon the independent contractor to ensure that they do follow the rules that set them apart from employees. You must not only be in business, you must do what businesses do. Be sure you have your own business cards, set up a website for your company and look after your accounting and legal records. When (not if) you have corporate meetings of the board and/or officers, be sure to prepare and maintain minutes of the meetings. You should also be sure to use a board meeting to authorize your annual salary and/ or dividends. This should be done, even if you are meeting with only yourself.

The ultimate success or failure of operating as an independent contractor rests with the astute management of your accumulating cash. The first hurdle is to understand that everything that you take in as income does not belong to you. Out of that money there are taxes and other liabilities, such as your accounting fees, that must be paid. Proper handling of your cash will ensure that you always have the funds available to meet these liabilities. Related to this is how much you take out of your company for your personal needs. Typically, an independent contractor does not need to draw as much income from his corporation as he was previously earning as an employee. Since the company will be paying a number of costs, normally paid from your net employment income and deducting them as a business expense, you don't require the same level of personal remuneration. It is imperative to leave money in your corporation to meet any contingencies, including gaps between contracts as well as using your corporation in a manner similar to creating your own RRSP.

The appropriate choice between salaries or dividends is a key step in ensuring that you are minimizing your taxes while managing your cash flow. As is typical with most contractors your cash reserves will grow rapidly and it is essential that you invest the funds appropriately. As noted in chapter 11 there are certain investments that will provide income that will be taxed more efficiently in your company than income from other types of investments. Getting to know and understand how the various types of income are taxed in your corporation will enable you to maximize your after-tax investment returns.

I hope you've enjoyed reading this book and haven't drifted off too often considering the technical nature of the content. I trust that you have a greater understanding of the opportunities and challenges faced by an independent contractor. I sincerely hope that this information will stand you in good stead should you decide to pursue this opportunity.

CHAPTER 13

The Contractor's Toolbox

There are a few "tools" that the independent contractor needs to have available to ease the burden he may face. To this end, a sample contract has been provided. The contract should be adapted to your particular situation and must follow the fundamentals for a good contract as set out in Chapter 8 of this book.

The other tools presented relate to your record keeping and your relationship with your accountant. A basic "chart of accounts" has been provided that indicates the primary general ledger accounts that you will need. In addition to the expense accounts set out in Chapter 7, the chart also lists asset, liability, equity and revenue accounts. Whether you use a commercial accounting package such as "QuickBooks" or "Simply Accounting" or perhaps a comprehensive spreadsheet as we provided to our clients, these accounts will need to be included.

What information do you need to provide to your accountant so that he can properly and efficiently prepare your yearend financial statements and tax returns? Two checklists have been provided to ensure that you present complete and accurate information to assist your accountant.

You will get better results if you work with a designated professional accountant that is experienced with working with independent contractors. Do not settle for someone who will just do the compliance work of preparing the statements and returns. You need an accountant that understands the nature of independent contracting work. To help you get the proper advice, a sample year end review meeting agenda has been provided. This sets out the matters to be addressed when you meet with your accountant to review the draft financial statements with him.

There are various lifestyle and life cycle issues that can and should be discussed with your accountant at least annually or periodically as events present themselves. This is where the experienced accountant will really earn his fee.

(DRAFT) CONTRACT FOR SERVICES AGREEMENT

BETWEEN

XXX Corporation,

("the Client")

–and–

SUBCONTRACTOR NAME

("the Contractor")

WHEREAS the Client is engaged in the business of providing xxxxxx xxxxxxx solutions to its clients;

AND WHEREAS the Contractor is engaged in the provision of xxxxxxxxx xxxxxxxxx technological services for the above type of company.

AND WHEREAS the Client wishes to retain the services of the Contractor and the Contractor has agreed to provide certain xxxxxxxxx xxxxxxxxx services;

NOW THEREFORE in consideration of the Client's willingness to retain the services of the Contractor and in further consideration of the mutual promises and covenants hereinafter set forth, the parties agree as follows:

SERVICES PROVIDED BY CONTRACTOR

1. The Contractor agrees to provide xxxxxxxxx xxxxxxxxx services and advice commensurate with the Contractor's education and experience, including the provision of in-house mentoring for the Client's staff, as the Client may request and the Contractor may accept from time to time during the term of this Agreement.

STATUS OF CONTRACTOR

2. The Contractor shall provide such services as an independent contractor and shall not be deemed to be an employee of the Client for any purposes at law whatsoever. The parties agree that this paragraph is of the essence in this Agreement.

OBLIGATIONS OF THE CONTRACTOR

Availability

3. The Contractor agrees to make himself/herself available to the Client at the Client's premises or other locations as required for the duration of this contract on a hourly basis as required by the Client. The contractor may provide a substitute individual subject to the client's approval and assessment of the replacement's qualifications to conduct the work as required to meet standards. The nature of this contract is to provide technical services on a (piece meal / hourly / daily) basis. The terms of this contract can be extended to other contracts or piecemeal jobs in the future in the absence of any new signed subcontractor agreement.

4. The Contractor is in no way restrained from deriving income from sources other than the Client, provided that the Contractor fulfills all contractual obligations pursuant to this Agreement.

Manner of Providing Services

5. In providing services as an independent contractor pursuant to the terms of this Agreement, the Contractor shall have full discretion as to the manner of providing services and shall render such services in accordance with the highest professional standards. However, the Contractor agrees to provide services pursuant to this Agreement in accordance with all applicable policies and standards as may be promulgated by the Client from time to time. In particular, standards applicable to standard conventions well know to the industry in which the company operates. In the event that the actions of the Contractor result in the scrapping, damage or similar loss, the Contractor agrees to reimburse, compensate and save harmless the Client from any additional costs incurred as a result of the Contractors negligence or lack of care.

Records and Reports

6. The Contractor agrees to maintain such records and reports (which are the property of the Client) as are required and specified by the Client. The Contractor agrees to provide appropriate security procedures for the protection and confidentiality of the aforementioned records and reports.

Remittances etc.

7. As an independent contractor, the Contractor is responsible for remitting all appropriate payments, taxes and assessments relating to Employment Insurance, Canada Pension Plan, Provincial Health, Provincial and Federal taxes, GST/HST, Workplace Safety and Insurance premiums, etc., to the proper authorities. The Contractor agrees to indemnify and save harmless the Client from and against all liability, costs, fines, claims or demands which may be made against the Client by reason of any failure on the part of the Client to withhold or

remit any of the aforementioned payments or any other tax, charge, premium, or payment from the remuneration paid to the Contractor as well as any costs or expense incurred in defending such claims or demands. Upon request, the Contractor will provide evidence of Workplace Safety and Insurance coverage to the Client.

Expenses

8. The Contractor shall be solely responsible for all expenses incurred by the Contractor related directly or indirectly to the performance of services pursuant to this agreement. Such expenses include, without limitation: professional dues, memberships fees; any fees or expense related to the Contractor's professional development, and continuing education (unless agreed otherwise); and any automotive, travel or other expenses incurred by the Contractor in the provision of services pursuant to this Agreement.

Authority

9. The Contractor shall have no authority to assume or create any obligation whatsoever, express or implied, in the name of the Client, except as expressly provided for in this Agreement. Further, the Contractor may not do any act or thing that would result in any liability or responsibility caused to the Client.

OBLIGATIONS OF THE COMPANY

Fee

10. The Client will pay the Contractor [XX.XX per piece ($XX.) per hour] for all hours properly invoiced.

Statement of Account

11. The Contractor shall provide the Company with an invoice or a statement of account on a regular basis detailing the number of hours worked and the services rendered. The Client shall pay the Contractor for services rendered pursuant

to this Agreement within 31 (days/weeks) of receipt by the Client of the applicable invoice or statement of account from the Contractor. A service charge of 2% per month accrued daily will be applicable for any late payments

Use of the Client's Property

12.   The Contractor shall be allowed to use tools, machines and other devices owned by the Client in the provision of services pursuant to this Agreement. In doing so, the Contractor agrees not to use the tools or other devices for any purpose other than that intended by the Client as outlined either verbally or in writing. All materials and devices will be returned to the Client immediately upon request. The Contractor will also, agree to supply and use their own tools and toolboxes while performing this contract. It is agreed that these tools and toolboxes supplied by the Contractor remain the assets of the Contractor at all times. At the completion of the piecemeal terms of this contract or at any time, the contractor may remove these tools that he/she has used to perform the services under this contract from the Client's premises.

CONFIDENTIALITY

13.   The Contractor may, in the process of providing services pursuant to this Agreement, be exposed to information and documentation about certain matters which are confidential to the Client and not known to the public or to competitors (hereinafter called "Confidential Materials , Information, Processes, Designs , Ideas and similar"). Such Confidential Materials , Information, Processes, Designs , Ideas and similar includes: all data, materials, products, technology, computer programs, specifications, manuals, business plans, software, marketing plans, business plans, financial information, and other information disclosed or submitted, orally, in writing, or by any other media, to the Contractor by the Client. Further-

more, the contractor agrees that any claim or possible claim regarding any tax credits, incentive, refunds, intellectual or patentable property, product or service remains the exclusive property of the Client indefinitely. In the event that there is any dispute, the contractor agrees to relinquish any claim or possible claim in favour of the Client for the compensation already earned and received based upon properly invoiced services submitted for payment to the Client as outlined in paragraph 10 above.

14.   The Contractor agrees that the Confidential Materials, Information, Processes, Designs , Ideas and similar are confidential and proprietary to the Client.

15.   The Contractor agrees to hold the Confidential Materials ,Information, Processes, Designs , Ideas and similar in confidence at all times, without time limitation, and shall not use the Confidential Materials , Information, Processes, Designs , Ideas and similar other than for the purpose of providing services pursuant to this Agreement, and shall disclose the Confidential Materials , Information, Processes, Designs , Ideas and similar only the Client's officers, directors, or employees with a specific need to know. The Contractor will not disclose, publish or otherwise reveal any of the Confidential Materials, Information, Processes, Designs, and Ideas and similar received from the Client to any other party whatsoever except with the specific prior written authorization of the Client.

16.   The Contractor further agrees that the Contractor shall not, during or after the term of this Agreement, make use of for the Contractor's or any third party's benefit any part of the Confidential Materials ,Information, Processes, Designs , Ideas and similar.

17.   The Contractor acknowledges that, in the event of any dispute as to whether information disclosed by the Contractor to a third party, or otherwise used by the Contractor, is Confidential Materials , Information, Processes, Designs , Ideas and similar, the onus shall be on the both parties equally

to demonstrate that it is not Confidential Materials , Information, Processes, Designs , Ideas and similar.

18. In the event of termination of this Agreement, whether by the Contractor or by the Client, the Contractor shall deliver to the Client all documents and data pertaining to Confidential Materials , Information, Processes, Designs , Ideas and similar and shall not remove any such documents or data of any kind which contain such Confidential Materials , Information, Processes, Designs , Ideas and similar.

NON-SOLICITATION

19. The Contractor acknowledges that during the course of the Contractor's engagement with the Client, the Contractor will develop a close working relationship with the Client 's customers and clients, gain a knowledge of the Client's methods of operation, trade secrets, processes, designs and acquire and be exposed to Confidential Materials , Information, Processes, Designs , Ideas and similar, all of which would cause irreparable harm and injury to the Client if made available to the competitor or if used for competitive purposes. Accordingly, the Contractor agrees that:

19.a for a period of six (6) months following the termination of this Agreement, regardless of how that termination should occur, the Contractor will not directly or indirectly solicit business from any client or customer or potential client or customer of the Company which was serviced or solicited by the Client or by the Contractor for the Client during the term of this Agreement at any time within the Province of (Ontario) and a 25 kilometre radius, and

19.b for a period of six (6) months following the termination of this Agreement, regardless of how that termination should occur, the Contractor shall not, on the Contractor's own behalf or on behalf of any entity with whom the Contractor is at the time associated, related, affiliated or employed by directly, or indirectly hire or offer to hire or entice away or in any other manner persuade or attempt to persuade any officer, agent, supplier, distributor or customer of the Client to discontinue or alter any one of their or its relationship(s) with the Client.

20. The Contractor agrees and acknowledges that the foregoing time and geographic limitations are reasonable and properly required for the adequate protection of the exclusive property and business of the Client, and in the event that any such time or geographic limitation is found to be unreasonable by a court, the duration or scope of the provision, as the case may be, shall be reduced so that the provisions becomes enforceable and, in its reduced form.

INJUNCTIVE RELIEF

21. The Contractor specifically acknowledges and agrees that the confidentiality and non solicitation restrictions contained in this Agreement are reasonable in view of the nature of the business in which the Client is engaged and the nature of the services provided by the Contractor pursuant to this Agreement. The Contractor hereby waives all defenses to the strict enforcement of the covenants contained in this Agreement by the Client. The Contractor further acknowledges, agrees, and understands that, without prejudice to any and all remedies available to the Client, an injunction is the only effective remedy for any breach of the confidentiality or non-solicitation covenants in this Agreement, and that the Client would suffer irreparable harm and injury in the event of any such breach. Accordingly, the Contractor hereby agrees that the Client may apply for and have injunctive relief, including an interim or interlocutory injunction, in any Court of com-

petent jurisdiction to enforce any of the confidentiality and/
or non-solicitation provisions in this Agreement upon the
breach or threatened breach thereof. The Contractor further
agrees that the Client may apply for and it is entitled to court
awarded costs and expenses, including reasonable legal costs.

TERM OF AGREEMENT

22.   Subject, to paragraph 24, below, this Agreement shall only
continue in full force and effect until "DATE." For added
certainty, and without limiting the generality of the foregoing, the Contractor acknowledges, understands and agrees
that unless the Client and the Contractor enter into any new
contract for services agreement, the contractual relationship
between the Client and the Contractor will fully and automatically expire on "DATE."

23.   The Client and the Contractor agree that this Agreement
may be terminated prior to "DATE" as follows:

23.a by the Client, at any time and without notice, for cause.
For the purpose of this Agreement, the Contractor
acknowledges that "cause" includes, with limitation,
any breach of this Agreement by the Contractor or any
failure by the Contractor to comply with the policies
and procedures promulgated by the Client from time to
time; or

23.b by the Client or the Contractor, at any time and for any
reason whatsoever, upon providing fourteen (14) days
advance written notice to the other party.

MISCELLANEOUS

24.   This Agreement shall be governed by and interpreted in
accordance with the laws of the Province of (Manitoba),

Canada.

25.   Should any provision of this Agreement be determined to be unenforceable, the invalidity in whole or in part of any such provision shall not affect the remaining provisions of this Agreement which shall continue to remain in full force and effect. Waiver by either party of any provision of this Agreement shall not continue a waiver as to any other instance, and any such waiver shall be in writing.

26.   This Agreement is not assignable by either party.

27.   Both parties agree that the contractor and the client has obtained, or had an opportunity to obtain, independent legal advice regarding the execution of this Agreement.

28.   Any notice required to be given pursuant to this Agreement shall be given by either party to the other in person or in writing to the following;

To the Client:	Address
	City, Province
	Postal Code
	Attn:
To the Contractor:	Address
	City, Province
	Postal Code

This Agreement shall be effective as of and from the XX day of Month, 20XX.

IN WITNESS WHEREOF the parties have duly executed this Agreement this _____ day of _____, _____ in the City of _____ in the Province of (Manitoba).

_____)

_____)

_____) _____

Witness   XXX Corporation

_____) Per:

_____)

_____)

_____) _____

Witness)   Contractor

CHART OF ACCOUNTS FOR THE INDEPENDENT CONTRACTOR

Suggested Chart of Accounts

In terms of accounting, a chart of accounts is simply a list of categories in which to record particular types of transactions.

The following suggested chart of accounts provides the independent contractor with perhaps the majority of accounts they will need to maintain their accounting records. The accounts indicate particular account numbers as well as a description of the content of the account. These suggested account numbers relate to the chart of accounts that was used by my clients, however you are free to use whatever numbering system is convenient for you. You should note that the numbering of the accounts may be determined by the particular software that you use. Some of the programs will require four digits or more. Again, the numbering is not important as much as the descriptions of the account's and your consistency in recording certain transactions into certain accounts.

Here are five overall classifications for the types of accounts that you will be using. The first three relate to accounts that will be found on your corporate balance sheet. These accounts are classified as assets, liabilities and shareholder equity. The last two classifications relate to accounts that will be found on your corporate income statement. The statement may also be referred to as the profit and loss statement. These accounts are classified as revenues and as expense accounts.

In some cases, the changes in the retained earnings may be reflected at the bottom of the income statement. In this case, the statement is generally titled statement of income and retained earnings. The closing balance of retained earnings is still carried forward and reported on the balance sheet.

As you use the chart of accounts, you may find that you need to add certain accounts, it which case you should try to enter them with numbering that will place the account in a logical area. You may also find that you are not using certain accounts at all, in which case you may want to simply delete the Accounts.

INDEPENDENT CONTRACTOR
BASIC CHART OF ACCOUNTS

ASSET ACCOUNTS:

100 thru 102 CASH & BANK

This is where you record the transactions that go through the bank accounts. It is important to reconcile the bank account monthly to ensure all items are recorded.

105 SHORT TERM INVESTMENTS

Record the cost of all short-term investments. Dividends re-invested will add to the cost base of your investments.

120 ACCOUNTS RECEIVABLE

This account is used at year-end to reflect the income earned and not received as at the year-end date. This includes work that may or may not have already been invoiced.

130 PREPAID EXPENSE

This account is used at year-end to record expenses paid in the current year that relate to the next fiscal period. For example insurance is expensed according to the passage of time.

140 INVENTORY

If you have purchased goods for resale, the cost value of the goods unsold at the fiscal year-end is recorded here.

150 DIRECTORS' ADVANCES

This account is the accumulation of drawings you have taken during the year and expenses paid on your behalf by the company, net of company expenses you have paid on behalf of the company and remuneration to you in the form of salaries or dividends. Consider this account acts like a bank account.

LONG TERM INVESTMENTS
180 AUTO LOAN
181 HOME LOAN

The auto loan and the home loan are special circumstances where you are permitted to borrow from the company in your capacity as an employee. A special resolution is required to authorize these loans and they are subject to specific rates and terms of repayment.

183 OTHER

General long-term investments are recorded in this account and may include investments in other private companies or investments in real estate.

CAPITAL ASSETS AND ACCUMULATED DEPRECIATION
190 AUTOMOBILE & 195 ACCUM DEPREC
200 COMPUTER HARDWARE & 205 ACCUM DEPREC
210 COMPUTER SOFTWARE & 215 ACCUM DEPREC
230 OFFICE EQUIPMENT & 235 ACCUM DEPREC
240 OFFICE FURNITURE & 245 ACCUM DEPREC

Expenditures on the above items having a life extending beyond the current fiscal year are recorded as assets if their cost exceeds $200. These assets are depreciated over the useful life or often at the rates prescribed for tax purposes. We generally do this calculation for our clients and record the depreciation/amortization expense and the accumulated amounts. Items costing less than $200 excluding GST should be recorded as a supply rather than as a capital asset.

LIABILITY ACCOUNTS:
300 ACCOUNTS PAYABLE

Includes expenditures incurred but not yet paid as at the fiscal year end. There is typically minimal amounts owing but it recording the payable allows a deduction before the amount is paid.

301 ACCRUED LIABILITIES

This account includes expenditures, which have not been billed to you as at the year-end, but the expense has been incurred by the passage of time. The annual accounting fees are an example.

310 GST PAYABLE

This is the amount charged on your invoices less the GST paid (ITC – input tax credits) on purchases. If using the "Quick Method" for GST, record the amounts charged on your invoice and the ITCs paid on capital assets. Your accountant will calculate the GST sundry revenue and reallocate it to the revenue account.

320 DIRECTOR'S FEES PAYABLE

This is the accrued salary allocated to a director but not paid as at the fiscal year end. We usually record this for you.

330 FEDERAL CORPORATE TAXES PAYABLE
331 PROVINCIAL CORPORATE TAXES PAYABLE

These accounts represent the liability at year-end for corporate income taxes. Record all payments and refunds in these accounts and provide us with all correspondence.

350 SHAREHOLDER LOANS

Enter all transactions with shareholders, who are not also a director of the company, such as drawings and items paid on behalf of the shareholder or company expenditures made by the shareholder.

360 BANK LOAN PAYABLE

Record any loans with your bank in this account. We need the details of the term, security and interest rate.

400 LONG TERM DEBTS

Record all debts that are of a long-term nature. We need the details of the term, security and interest rate.

SHAREHOLDER EQUITY ACCOUNTS:

500 ISSUED CAPITAL

Record the issuance of shares at cost in this account. Share capital represents ownership of the company and is essential.

510 RETAINED EARNINGS (DEFICIT)

This is the net worth of your company and represents the earnings not paid out to the shareholders as at the year-end. Your objective is to maximize this account.

520 DIVIDENDS PAID

Record the dividends declared during the current fiscal year. Prior year dividends are closed out to the retained earnings account.

525 REFUNDABLE TAXES PAID (RECOVERED)

Certain taxes paid on investment income may be potentially refundable as and are charged to equity. The recovery of these taxes is also recorded in this account.

<u>Note:</u>

The accounts above are reported on your balance sheet. They reflect what you own which are your asset accounts, what you owe which are your liability accounts and the result of the equation assets minus liabilities is the shareholder equity. With an independent contractor Corporation, the shareholder equity is a reasonable estimate of the company's net worth. The objective of this game is to maximize the net worth.

The following accounts are reported on your income statement. They reflect the income that you generated during your fiscal year end and the expenses you have incurred to earn that income. The formula here is revenue minus expenses equals net income before taxes. The corporate income taxes are calculated starting with the net income before taxes. There will be some reconciliation between the accounting income and income for tax purposes.

REVENUE ACCOUNTS:

600 CONTRACT INCOME

Record all invoices issued for services earned during the fiscal year, including the date of the invoice and the date the invoice was deposited in the corporate bank account. Show the net amount of the invoice (excluding GST) and the GST charged in separate columns. Any outstanding invoices at year end will appear on the balance sheet as Accounts Receivable.

601 FOREIGN CONTRACT REVENUE

Revenue earned outside Canada must be converted and reported in Canadian funds. Please record foreign income indicating the amount invoiced in foreign currency and the Canadian equivalent. If the Corporation is earning foreign income it will not be collecting GST on that income, therefore it must be recorded separately. Your accountant can do the conversion to Canadian funds for you using the conversion rates set by Revenue Canada each year.

605 REIMBURSED EXPENSES

Record reimbursements here that are more like an allowance and don't relate to any specific expenditure. Reimbursements of specific items should be netted with the expenditure.

610 GST SUNDRY INCOME

GST Sundry Income results when using the "Quick" method of reporting GST. It is the difference between the GST collected and the amount of GST that is payable to the Receiver General. The "Quick" method may only be used when earned revenue is below $200,000 including GST annually. Depending on your province, GST might be replaced with GST/HST.

OTHER INCOME

615 DIVIDEND INCOME

620 INTEREST INCOME

625 CAPITAL GAINS (LOSSES)

628 FOREIGN EXCHANGE GAINS (LOSSES)

630 OTHER

Record details of all other income earned by the Corporation up to and including the year-end. This includes any dividends and capital gains or losses from stock or mutual fund investments, as well as bank interest and GIC interest. Indicate if the dividend is from a Canadian security. Each type of investment income serves a different purpose on the tax return, please specify which type of income it is, and record each type separately.

EXPENSE ACCOUNTS:

700 ACCOUNTING FEES

701 ACCOUNTING FEES - OTHER

Record fees for accounting services or retainers in account 700, and record other accounting or bookkeeping fees in Account

701. Include the names of the parties to whom other payments were made.

710 ADVERTISING

Record expenses such as media advertising, gifts purchased for clients and any expenses related to image (advertising done through your personal appearance). This includes business suits and accessories and their dry cleaning, expenses for personal grooming. Include sponsorships or donations where a tax receipt is not provided.

720 AUTOMOBILE EXPENSE

Keep a log book for each vehicle indicating the total kilometers driven and the kilometers driven to earn income. We advise clients to keep automobiles in their personal name to avoid taxable benefits being charged.

Method 1- Calculate the percentage that an auto is used for business purposes to determine the amount allowable as an expense. Record each vehicle's expenses separately into categories such as fuel, repairs and parts, license and registration fees, insurance, general maintenance (oil changes), leasing costs (subject to a maximum) and interest on auto loans. A lease down payment will be set up as a prepaid expense and expensed over the lease period. You may claim amortization on automobiles owned personally. Provide the value of the car at the beginning of the fiscal year.

Provide a copy of the bill of sale for a new purchase.

Method 2 - provides for a car allowance based on kilometers driven for business at the prescribed rates as set by Canada Revenue Agency each year.

Both methods need to be calculated, and the one resulting in a higher expense is the one to claim.

730 BANK CHARGES

Record the cost of all bank charges, including costs of printing cheques, credit card annual fees and safety deposit box charges, in this account. Brokerage fees should be added to the cost of investments, not expensed as bank charges.

740 BOOKS AND PERIODICALS

Include costs of books, magazines, newspapers, and videos that assist you in any way with your business.

750 BUSINESS PROMOTION

Record 100% of all meal and entertainment expenses incurred for actual or potential clients. Include expenses such as business meals and entertainment, including the cost of food and drink if entertaining clients at home, gratuities and cover charges, tickets to entertainment or sporting events including private boxes and room rental to provide entertainment. CRA allows only 50% of meal and entertainment expenses to be deducted as they feel individuals are receiving some personal benefit. All amounts included will be reduced by 50% on the corporate tax return. Golfing fees and memberships in any primarily recreational club are not tax deductible but should be recorded as a business expense as long as they serve a business purpose. Up to six "events" per year are 100% deductible if all employees are allowed to attend such as a Christmas party.

760 COMPUTER SUPPLIES

Computer supplies would include hardware and software items under $200, CD/DVDs, printer ribbons or toner cartridges, printer paper, and computer club charges (e.g. facebook/twitter expenses).

770 CONSULTING FEES

Record payments made to subcontractors.

780 AMORTIZATION (DEPRECIATION)

Amortization is a method of writing off the cost of a capital asset over its useful life. The amount deducted each year is based on the unamortized cost from the prior year. Your accountant will calculate the amortization once we have determined the value of the assets.

790 DIRECTORS FEES

If applicable, we will record the directors' fee expense after calculation your salary/dividend mix and allocation for the year.

800 EDUCATION AND SEMINARS

Record costs of courses taken or seminars attended. A maximum of two conventions per year may be claimed provided they are business related.

810 EMPLOYEE BENEFITS

Record the employer's share of CPP that you have paid during the year.

820 GENERAL EXPENSES

Record any small incidental expenses that do not fit into any other category in the General Expense Account.

As a rule, the general expense category should remain at zero, or as close to it as possible, to avoid any red flags.

830 INSURANCE

Include amounts paid for commercial insurance on buildings and equipment as well as health and dental premiums paid to a group plan. Do not deduct disability premiums, as any disability benefits will then be taxable. Life insurance premiums are not tax deductible.

840 INTEREST & PENALTIES

Interest paid on money borrowed to earn income is deductible. Penalties and/or interest incurred on government remittances is not deductible for tax purposes but should be recorded for book-keeping purposes.

850 OFFICE SUPPLIES

Record the cost of items such as printing, stationery, postage, delivery, paper, pens, pencils and general office supplies. Office equipment or furniture costing less than $200 before tax should also be included here.

860 PROFESSIONAL FEES

Record any legal or professional fees paid which may assist the Corporation in earning income. The incorporation fee as well as memberships in professional and other associations should be included here.

870 RENT

Rent paid for property leased by the corporation may be deducted as Rent Expense. Clients with a home office should also record 100% of home office expenses such as heat, hydro, water, mortgage interest, home insurance, property taxes or rent, landscaping, lawn care, snow removal, repairs and maintenance and decorating as Rent Expense. Calculate the percentage allowable by taking the amount of space used for the home office versus the total living space of the home. Do not forget to include the garage if the car is used for business.

880 REPAIRS & MAINTENANCE

Record repairs of a strictly business nature which are not included as part of home or auto expenses, such as computer and equipment repairs, and installation of electrical or telephone jacks in the office portion of the home.

890 TELEPHONE

Record expenses for cellular phones and on-line or Internet services as well as long distance calls for business made from the home telephone. Note that basic residential service is not deductible but a separate business line is.

900 TRAVEL

Record all business travel expenses such as plane, train, taxi, public transportation, hotel accommodations and parking. Travel expenses to attend conventions or seminars should be included here as well.

950 WAGES AND BENEFITS

Record wages paid to any employees who are not directors of the Corporation. Clients should note that their spouse and children can be hired as employees.

Year-End Information Checklist

The best way to minimize your accounting fees is to ensure that your accountant receives complete and accurate information on a timely basis. Missing or incomplete information will cause inefficiencies and more time will be added to your file. For a "Notice to Reader" engagement the following is the basic information needed to complete your fiscal year end in a timely and efficient manner. If additional information is required, your accountant will contact you. Provide the following documentation and complete the **"Additional Information Year End Checklist"** form in full and take it to your accountant's office with all the necessary information to prepare all your year-end documents.

Documentation required:

In order to prepare your annual financial statements and corporate tax returns, we require the following:

- ☐ The completed Spreadsheet if applicable. If you are using a commercial accounting program in lieu of the completed spreadsheet, please provide a backup disk and a printout of the General Ledger, Balance Sheet & Income Statement along with the remaining items. (The above items can be sent via email)
- ☐ Corporate bank statements and cancelled cheques for the **full** fiscal year for all corporate accounts. If available, please also provide the statement for the month following your fiscal year end. Include the bank reconciliation if you have it.
- ☐ Copies of Canada Revenue Agency's (CRA) statements showing any source deductions sent in during the year.
- ☐ Working copies of GST/HST returns filed for the year, including assessments received showing any interest/penalties charged during the year.
- ☐ Copies of federal and provincial "Notices of Assessment" for the previous taxation year.
- ☐ If instalments were paid, a copy of "Statement of Account" from both the federal and provincial (where applicable) governments showing total instalments paid for the year.
- ☐ Copies of statements for any brokerage accounts maintained in the company's name for the year end period. (Our accountant's staff generally provide the bookkeeping for these

accounts)

- ☐ Copies of any term deposit certificates, which were taken out or matured during the year-end period.
- ☐ Your minute book.
- ☐ A copy of all invoices for the acquisition of fixed assets.
- ☐ Any other information you feel will help your accountant complete your year-end such as information with respect to your personal income and deductions available for the current calendar year as well as your preference for salary or dividends.
- ☐ Have you acquired a new car or a new home this year?
- ☐ Have you filed the "Annual Return?" (Yes/No)

Please also complete the "Additional Information Year End Checklist."

Additional Information Year End Checklist

The following is generally information to be reported on your tax returns. It is also information that may change from time to time, so this checklist should be completed annually to put the onus on your accountant to get the information properly on your returns.

(complete Each item or mark as not applicable (n/a) – do not leave blank**)**

- ☐ Name of Company:
- ☐ Name of Client: Contact:
- ☐ Fiscal Year End (date): ___   ☐ GST/HST Method (Quick or Long):
- ☐ Head Office: _____   ☐ Postal Code:
- ☐ Mailing Address: _   ☐ Postal Code:
- ☐ Bus: ( ) ☐ Res: ( ) ☐ Fax: ( )
- ☐ Email: ___   ☐ Date of incorporation:
- ☐ Provincial Account Number: ___   ☐ Business Number:
- ☐ Type of Business: _____   ☐ Percent of Total Income:
- ☐ Name & S.I.N. of each Director

_____   SIN

_____   SIN

_____   SIN

☐ Types and number of shares issued (from the minute book)

Type of Share	Number Authorized	Number Issued	Total Value	Issued To	SIN

Toolbox Figure 1: Share certificate table

☐ Do you require any of the following additional services:

Preparation of T1's (for personal tax returns)

☐ Yes   ☐ No

Preparation of T4's (for director's fees or wages paid)

☐ Yes   ☐ No

Preparation of T5's for dividends paid

☐ Yes   ☐ No

Year End Review Meeting Agenda

FINANCIAL STATEMENT ACCURACY:

The objective is to ensure that the financial and tax figures are correct and that you, the client have a reasonable understanding of the content of the financial statements. The steps are as follows:

1. Review the financial statements to ensure that they are what you had anticipated.
2. Comparison of your results to what you expected and to some relevant benchmarking.
3. Resolve any apparent errors.
4. Determine or confirm the salary/dividends for the current year.
5. Discuss payment of balances of tax.

6. Discuss tax instalments for the coming year; corporate and GST/HST.
7. Confirm if you want your accountant to prepare, T1, T4, and/ or T5. (Recommended)
8. Discuss any potential areas for improvement in submitting data to your accountant.

Tax And Financial Planning:

The objective is to ensure that you have covered any tax or salary/ dividend issues coming out of the statement review and discuss any financial and planning matters that may be of concern to you. The steps are as follows:

Review items noted for discussion on the Financial Issues Document covering areas such as:

> Marketing
> Cash Flow Planning
> Tax Planning
> Investment Planning
> Risk Management
> Retirement and Estate Planning

Completion Planning:

1. Estimate date when file will be complete for filing returns (consider deadlines)
2. Discuss payment options and estimate when invoice will be prepared.
3. Any other matter that you want to discuss with your accountant.

Financial Issues Document For The Independent Contractor

Client Issues	Yes	No	N/A
Record Keeping:			
•Accurate			
•Complete			
•Accountant did bookkeeping			
•Computerized (Quickbooks, Simply Acctg, Excel, Other?)			
Marketing:			
•Currently contracting?			
•Networking			
•Skill set and upgrading?			
•Potential windup of company?			
Cash Flow Planning:			
•Excess cash to be put to work			
•Consider three pools required			
•Family spending habits (budgeting)			
•Bankruptcy?			
Tax Planning:			
•Salary/dividend/consulting fee			
•Income splitting with spouse			
•Income splitting with children or parents			
•Convert employee to contractor			
•Taxation of property/investment income			
•Maximize business expenses			

•Home/auto loans			
•Acquire audit insurance			
Investment Planning:			
•Establish goals			
•Consider risks			
•Investment vehicles			
•Registered vs. unregistered plans (Retirement)			
•Using the company as long term RRSP			
•Minimize directors' advances			
•Investing for Education			
•Investing in Real Estate			
Risk Management:			
•Holding company?			
•Life, disability & health			
•Home & auto coverage			
•Professional and general liability coverage			
Retirement and Estate Planning:			
•Net worth assessment			
•Retirement income plans and pensions			
•Non-financial considerations			
•Probate, Intestacy			
•Wills & powers of attorney			
•Charitable donations			
•Estate Freeze			

Life Changes:			
•Starting out: Your first job			
•Changing jobs or careers			
•Getting married			
•Buying a home			
•Having Children			
•Starting a small business			
•Caring for Aging Parents			
•Divorcing			
•Receiving a Windfall			
•Retiring			
Other Matters:			
•Our work comes from client referrals; can client accommodate?			
•Can client provide us with a testimonial			
•Completion of the "Quality Service Questionnaire"			

Schedule 1 – Employee Contractor Comparisons – British Columbia Tax Rates

Schedule 1A – Employee Contractor Comparisons – British Columbia Tax Rates

Schedule 2 – Employee Contractor Comparisons – Manitoba Tax Rates

Schedule 2A – Employee Contractor Comparisons – Manitoba Tax Rates

Schedule 3 – Employee Contractor Comparisons – Ontario Tax Rates

Schedule 3A – Employee Contractor Comparisons – Ontario Tax Rates

Schedule 4 – Employee Contractor Comparisons – Newfoundland Tax Rates

Schedule 4A – Employee Contractor Comparisons – Newfoundland Tax Rates

Schedule 5 – Proprietorship/Corporation Comparisons – British Columbia Tax Rates

Schedule 6 – Proprietorship/Corporation Comparisons – Manitoba Tax Rates

Schedule 7 – Proprietorship/Corporation Comparisons – Ontario Tax Rates

Schedule 8 – Proprietorship/Corporation Comparisons – Newfoundland Tax Rates

Employee Contractor Comparisons – British Columbia Tax Rates

The following analysis expands the comparison of the net after-tax income of an employee versus an incorporated independent contractor using the 2013 personal and corporate tax rates. Consider this as a comparison of the same individual working as an employee versus working as an incorporated contractor.

We have used the same assumptions as set out in Chapter 2, where there is a 33% variance between the salary earned by an employee as compared to the gross revenue generated by a contractor. In the following example, the contractor is able to split a salary with his spouse on the assumption that she has no other income.

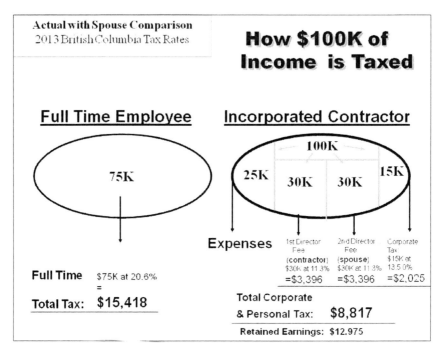

Figure 1: BC comp with spouse

In the above example, the full time employee is paid a salary of $75,000 and pays $15,418 in personal income tax leaving a take home pay of $59,582. Out of the take-home pay he must still pay about 85% of the expenses that the independent contractor has deducted pre-tax. The employee is therefore left with about $38,332 to use for lifestyle and investment purposes.

The contractor and his spouse each have $26,604 left from their salaries (total $53,208) to meet their lifestyle and investment purposes plus the company still has $12,975 left which can also be invested. The contractor therefore has about $66,182 left compared to $38,332 for the employee.

This is 72.7% more after-tax income for the contractor!

Future Value: The contractor has $27,851 more per year available than does the employee. Invested at 2.75% for 25 years this savings would amount to about $982,746.

Employee Contractor Comparisons – British Columbia Tax Rates

We have used the same assumptions as set out in Chapter 2, where there is a 33% variance between the salary earned by an employee as compared to the gross revenue generated by a contractor. Consider this as a comparison of the same individual working as an employee versus working as an incorporated contractor.

In the following example, the contractor is not able to split a salary with a spouse on the assumption that she has too much other income or the contractor is not married. When the contractor is single or has a spouse that works outside the home, it may not be possible or practical for the contractor to fully split the income. Even in one of these situations, there is a significant financial advantage to be an independent contractor as the income can be split with the corporation to take advantage of the low corporate tax rates.

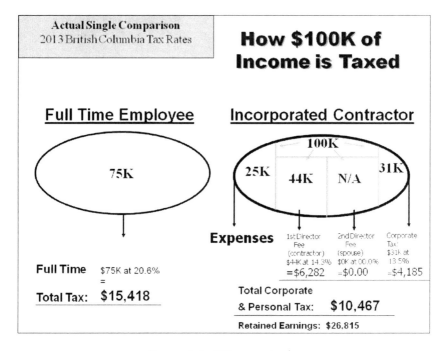

Figure 1A: BC rates single

In the above example, the full time employee is paid a salary of $75,000 and pays $15,418 in personal income tax leaving a take home pay of $59,582. Out of the take-home pay he must still pay about 85% of the expenses that the independent contractor has deducted pre-tax. The employee is therefore left with about $38,332 to use for lifestyle and investment purposes.

In order to have approximately the same level of funds in hand as the employee, the individual contractor would take a salary of $44,000. The contractor has $37,718 left from his/her salary to meet lifestyle and investment purposes, plus the company still has $26,815 left which can also be invested. The contractor therefore has about $64,533 left compared to $38,332 for the employee. **This is 68.4% more after-tax income for the contractor!**

Future Value: The contractor has $26,201 more per year available than does the employee. Invested at 2.75% for 25 years this savings would amount to almost $924,525.

Employee Contractor Comparisons – Manitoba Tax Rates

The following analysis expands the comparison of the net after-tax income of an employee versus an incorporated independent contractor using the 2013 personal and corporate tax rates. Consider this as a comparison of the same individual working as an employee versus working as an incorporated contractor.

We have used the same assumptions as set out in Chapter 2, where there is a 33% variance between the salary earned by an employee as compared to the gross revenue generated by a contractor. In the following example, the contractor is able to split a salary with his spouse on the assumption that she has no other income.

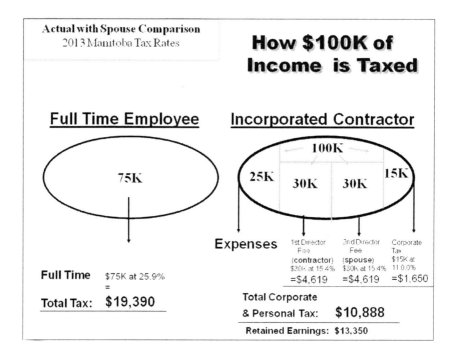

Figure 2: Manitoba rates with spouse

In the above example, the full time employee is paid a salary of $75,000 and pays $19,390 in personal income tax leaving a take home pay of $55,610. Out of the take-home pay he must still pay about 85% of the expenses that the independent contractor has deducted pre-tax. The employee is therefore left with about $34,360 to use for lifestyle and investment purposes.

The contractor and his spouse each have $25,381 left from their salaries (total $50,762) to meet their lifestyle and investment purposes plus the company still has $13,350 left which can also be invested. The contractor therefore has about $64,112 left compared to $34,360 for the employee.

This is 86.6% more after-tax income for the contractor!

Future Value: The contractor has $29,752 more per year available than does the employee. Invested at 2.75% for 25 years this savings would amount to about $1,049,825.

Employee Contractor Comparisons – Manitoba Tax Rates

We have used the same assumptions as set out in Chapter 2, where there is a 33% variance between the salary earned by an employee as compared to the gross revenue generated by a contractor. Consider this as a comparison of the same individual working as an employee versus working as an incorporated contractor.

In the following example, the contractor is not able to split a salary with a spouse on the assumption that she has too much other income or the contractor is not married. When the contractor is single or has a spouse that works outside the home, it may not be possible or practical for the contractor to fully split the income. Even in one of these situations, there is a significant financial advantage to be an independent contractor as the income can be split with the corporation to take advantage of the low corporate tax rates.

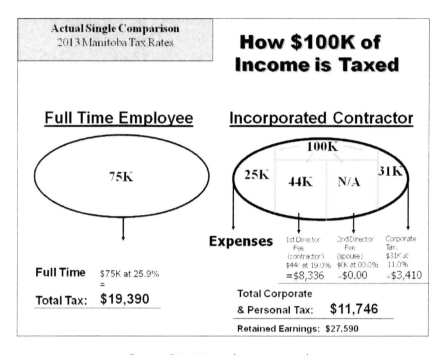

Figure 2A: Manitoba rates single

In the above example, the full time employee is paid a salary of $75,000 and pays $19,390 in personal income tax leaving a take home pay of $55,610. Out of the take-home pay he must still pay about 85% of the expenses that the independent contractor has deducted pre-tax. The employee is therefore left with about $34,360 to use for lifestyle and investment purposes.

In order to have approximately the same level of funds in hand as the employee, the individual contractor would take a salary of $44,000. The contractor has $35,664 left from his/her salary to meet lifestyle and investment purposes, plus the company still has $27,590 left which can also be invested. The contractor therefore has about $63,254 left compared to $34,360 for the employee. **This is 84.1% more after-tax income for the contractor!**

Future Value: The contractor has $28,894 more per year available than does the employee. Invested at 2.75% for 25 years this savings would amount to almost $1,019,549.

Employee Contractor Comparisons — Ontario Tax Rates

The following analysis expands the comparison of the net after-tax income of an employee versus an incorporated independent contractor using the 2013 personal and corporate tax rates. Consider this as a comparison of the same individual working as an employee versus working as an incorporated contractor.

We have used the same assumptions as set out in Chapter 2, where there is a 33% variance between the salary earned by an employee as compared to the gross revenue generated by a contractor. In the following example, the contractor is able to split a salary with his spouse on the assumption that she has no other income.

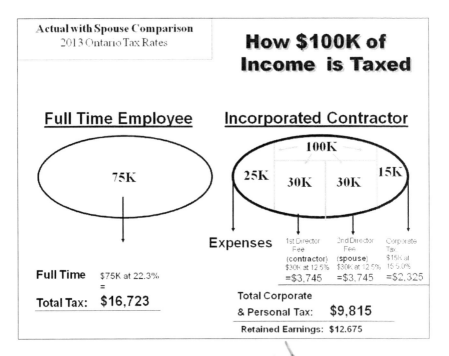

Figure 3: Ontario rates with spouse

In the above example, the full time employee is paid a salary of $75,000 and pays $16,723 in personal income tax leaving a take home pay of $58,277. Out of the take-home pay he must still pay about 85% of the expenses that the independent contractor has deducted pre-tax. The employee is therefore left with about $37,027 to use for lifestyle and investment purposes.

The contractor and his spouse each have $26,255 left from their salaries (total $52,510) to meet their lifestyle and investment purposes plus the company still has $12,675 left which can also be invested. The contractor therefore has about $65,185 left compared to $37,027 for the employee.

This is 76.1% more after-tax income for the contractor!

Future Value: The contractor has $28,158 more per year available than does the employee. Invested at 2.75% for 25 years this savings would amount to about $993,579.

Employee Contractor Comparisons – Ontario Tax Rates

We have used the same assumptions as set out in Chapter 2, where there is a 33% variance between the salary earned by an employee as compared to the gross revenue generated by a contractor. Consider this as a comparison of the same individual working as an employee versus working as an incorporated contractor.

In the following example, the contractor is not able to split a salary with a spouse on the assumption that she has too much other income or the contractor is not married. When the contractor is single or has a spouse that works outside the home, it may not be possible or practical for the contractor to fully split the income. Even in one of these situations, there is a significant financial advantage to be an independent contractor as the income can be split with the corporation to take advantage of the low corporate tax rates.

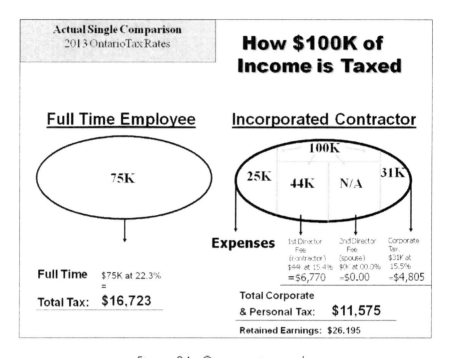

Figure 3A: Ontario rates single

In the above example, the full time employee is paid a salary of $75,000 and pays $16,723 in personal income tax leaving a take home pay of $58,277. Out of the take-home pay he must still pay about 85% of the expenses that the independent contractor has deducted pre-tax. The employee is therefore left with about $37,027 to use for lifestyle and investment purposes.

In order to have approximately the same level of funds in hand as the employee, the individual contractor would take a salary of $44,000. The contractor has $37,230 left from his/her salary to meet lifestyle and investment purposes, plus the company still has $26,195 left which can also be invested. The contractor therefore has about $63,425 left compared to $37,027 for the employee. **This is 71.3% more after-tax income for the contractor!**

Future Value: The contractor has $26,398 more per year available than does the employee. Invested at 2.75% for 25 years this savings would amount to almost $931,476.

Employee Contractor Comparisons — Newfoundland Tax Rates

The following analysis expands the comparison of the net after-tax income of an employee versus an incorporated independent contractor using the 2013 personal and corporate tax rates. Consider this as a comparison of the same individual working as an employee versus working as an incorporated contractor.

We have used the same assumptions as set out in Chapter 2, where there is a 33% variance between the salary earned by an employee as compared to the gross revenue generated by a contractor. In the following example, the contractor is able to split a salary with his spouse on the assumption that she has no other income.

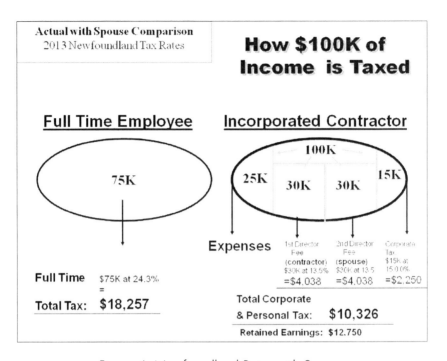

Figure 4: Newfoundland Rates with Spouse

In the above example, the full time employee is paid a salary of $75,000 and pays $18,257 in personal income tax leaving a take home pay of $56,743. Out of the take-home pay he must still pay about 85% of the expenses that the independent contractor has deducted pre-tax. The employee is therefore left with about $35,493 to use for lifestyle and investment purposes.

The contractor and his spouse each have $25,962 left from their salaries (total $51,924) to meet their lifestyle and investment purposes plus the company still has $12,750 left which can also be invested. The contractor therefore has about $64,674 left compared to $35,493 for the employee.

This is 82.2% more after-tax income for the contractor!

Future Value: The contractor has $29,181 more per year available than does the employee. Invested at 2.75% for 25 years this savings would amount to about $1,029,676.

Employee Contractor Comparisons – Newfoundland Tax Rates

We have used the same assumptions as set out in Chapter 2, where there is a 33% variance between the salary earned by an employee as compared to the gross revenue generated by a contractor. Consider this as a comparison of the same individual working as an employee versus working as an incorporated contractor.

In the following example, the contractor is not able to split a salary with a spouse on the assumption that she has too much other income or the contractor is not married. When the contractor is single or has a spouse that works outside the home, it may not be possible or practical for the contractor to fully split the income. Even in one of these situations, there is a significant financial advantage to be an independent contractor as the income can be split with the corporation to take advantage of the low corporate tax rates.

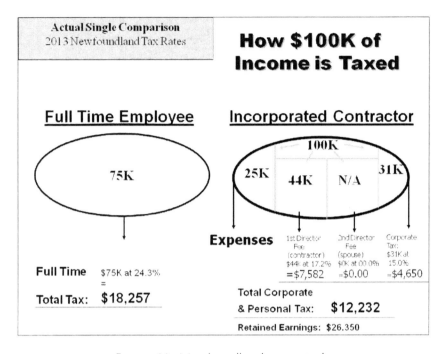

Figure 4A: Newfoundland rates single

In the above example, the full time employee is paid a salary of $75,000 and pays $18,257 in personal income tax leaving a take home pay of $56,743. Out of the take-home pay he must still pay about 85% of the expenses that the independent contractor has deducted pre-tax. The employee is therefore left with about $35,493 to use for lifestyle and investment purposes.

In order to have approximately the same level of funds in hand as the employee, the individual contractor would take a salary of $44,000. The contractor has $36,418 left from his/her salary to meet lifestyle and investment purposes, plus the company still has $26,350 left which can also be invested. The contractor therefore has about $62,768 left compared to $35,493 for the employee. **This is 76.9% more after-tax income for the contractor!**

Future Value: The contractor has $27,275 more per year available than does the employee. Invested at 2.75% for 25 years this savings would amount to almost $962,422.

Proprietorship/Corporation Comparisons – British Columbia Tax Rates

We will look at a comparison of earning gross contract revenue of $100,000 in British Columbia through a proprietorship and through a corporation. The assumptions and figures are similar to what we looked at in Chapter 2. To make the comparison as simple as possible we will make some assumptions as follows:

1. The gross revenue is $100,000 for both the proprietor and for the corporation. There is no rate differential if you operate either way unless you are contracting through a placement firm. Operating expenses total $20,000 of which $3,000 is for meals and entertainment. Such expenses are tax deductible at only 50% of the actual expenditure.

2. The tax rates in effect are those for British Columbia in 2013. As with the previous examples, we want to use flat rates for simplicity.

3. A salary is taken from the corporation set at $51,100 being the maximum level for 2013 CPP contributions. Please note that the CPP has been removed in the tax calculations below. As the salary for the incorporated contractor is set at the maximum for contributions, there should be no difference in the net tax between the two options.

4. No Registered Retirement Savings Plan contributions
   (RRSPs) are considered.

	Proprietorship	Corporation
Gross Revenue	$100,000	$100,000
Less:		
Expenses	20,000	20,000
Salary	NIL	51,100
Net Income	$80,000	$28,900
Taxable Income	$81,500	$30,400
TAXES:		
Personal Tax	$17,527	$8,320
Corporate Tax	NIL	4,104
Total Tax	$17,527	$12,424
Net for lifestyle and investments	$62,473	$67,576

Prop Figure 5: BC Proprietorship comparison table

The sole proprietor reports his net business income in his annual personal tax return and is taxed using the graduated tax brackets. The incorporated contractor can set his salary remuneration at any level required to meet his current lifestyle requirements. It is interesting to note that because the business is now paying for a lot of expenses that would be paid from after-tax income as an employee; a contractor does not require as high a salary as he had as an employee.

The British Columbia incorporated contractor pays himself a salary of $51,100 and after taxes of $8,320 still has a net of $42,780 from this source. In addition, the company still retains $24,796 that can be invested within the company.

In the above table we have used a salary for the incorporated contractor's remuneration rather than a dividend or a salary/dividend combination. Doing so would improve the incorporated contractor's position relative to the proprietor in most provinces. Even using a salary for the remuneration, there is still a distinct financial advantage for the incorporated contractor. As the gross and net revenues increase, the discrepancy will grow as more and more of the proprietor's income will be taxed at higher marginal personal tax rates.

In the simple example set out above, the net savings in taxes through a corporation operating in British Columbia is **$5,103 per year.**

Future Value of $5,296 per annum invested at a rate of 2.75%:

5 years	$ 26,957
10 years	$ 57,831
15 years	$ 93,190
25 years	$180,064

While artificial numbers have been used in the scenarios used here, my "average" incorporated independent contractor client in 2011 was grossing in excess of $130,000 and spending approximately $19,000 on expenses. The "average" figures are achieved by eliminating the top and bottom 20% of clients and using only the mid-sixty range.

SCHEDULE 6

Proprietorship/Corporation Comparisons – Manitoba Tax Rates

We will look at a comparison of earning gross contract revenue of $100,000 in Manitoba through a proprietorship and through a corporation. The assumptions and figures are similar to what we looked at in Chapter 2. To make the comparison as simple as possible we will make some assumptions as follows:

1. The gross revenue is $100,000 for both the proprietor and for the corporation. There is no rate differential if you operate either way unless you are contracting through a placement firm. Operating expenses total $20,000 of which $3,000 is for meals and entertainment. Such expenses are tax deductible at only 50% of the actual expenditure.

2. The tax rates in effect are those for Manitoba in 2013. As with the previous examples, we want to use flat rates for simplicity.

3. A salary is taken from the corporation set at $51,100 being the maximum level for 2013 CPP contributions. Please note that the CPP has been removed in the tax calculations below. As the salary for the incorporated contractor is set at the maximum for contributions, there should be no difference in the net tax between the two options.

4. No Registered Retirement Savings Plan contributions (RRSPs) are considered.

	Proprietorship	Corporation
Gross Revenue	$100,000	$100,000
Less:		
Expenses	20,000	20,000
Salary	NIL	51,100
Net Income	$80,000	$28,900
Taxable Income	$81,500	$30,400
TAXES:		
Personal Tax	$21,951	$10,713
Corporate Tax	NIL	3,344
Total Tax	$21,951	$14,057
Net for lifestyle and investments	$58,049	$65,943

Prop Figure 6: Manitoba Proprietorship comparison table

The sole proprietor reports his net business income in his annual personal tax return and is taxed using the graduated tax brackets. The incorporated contractor can set his salary remuneration at any level required to meet his current lifestyle requirements. It is interesting to note that because the business is now paying for a lot of expenses that would be paid from after-tax income as an employee; a contractor does not require as high a salary as he had as an employee.

The Manitoba incorporated contractor pays himself a salary of $51,100 and after taxes of $10,713 still has a net of $40,387 from this source. In addition, the company still retains $25,556 that can be invested within the company.

In the above table we have used a salary for the incorporated contractor's remuneration rather than a dividend or a salary/dividend combination. Doing so would improve the incorporated contractor's position relative to the proprietor in most provinces. Even using a salary for the remuneration, there is still a distinct financial advantage for the incorporated contractor. As the gross and net revenues increase, the discrepancy will grow as more and more of the proprietor's income will be taxed at higher marginal personal tax rates.

In the simple example set out above, the net savings in taxes through a corporation operating in Manitoba is **$7,894 per year.**

Future Value of $7,894 per annum invested at a rate of 2.75%:

5 years	$ 41,701
10 years	$ 89,461
15 years	$ 144,158
25 years	$278,546

While artificial numbers have been used in the scenarios used here, my "average" incorporated independent contractor client in 2011 was grossing in excess of $130,000 and spending approximately $19,000 on expenses. The "average" figures are achieved by eliminating the top and bottom 20% of clients and using only the mid-sixty range.

Proprietorship/Corporation Comparisons – Ontario Tax Rates

We will look at a comparison of earning gross contract revenue of $100,000 in Ontario through a proprietorship and through a corporation. The assumptions and figures are similar to what we looked at in Chapter 2. To make the comparison as simple as possible we will make some assumptions as follows:

1. The gross revenue is $100,000 for both the proprietor and for the corporation. There is no rate differential if you operate either way unless you are contracting through a placement firm. Operating expenses total $20,000 of which $3,000 is for meals and entertainment. Such expenses are tax deductible at only 50% of the actual expenditure.

2. The tax rates in effect are those for Ontario in 2013. As with the previous examples, we want to use flat rates for simplicity.

3. A salary is taken from the corporation set at $51,100 being the maximum level for 2013 CPP contributions. Please note that the CPP has been removed in the tax calculations below. As the salary for the incorporated contractor is set at the maximum for contributions, there should be no difference in the net tax between the two options.

4. No Registered Retirement Savings Plan contributions

(RRSPs) are considered.

	Proprietorship	Corporation
Gross Revenue	$100,000	$100,000
Less:		
Expenses	20,000	20,000
Salary	NIL	51,100
Net Income	$80,000	$28,900
Taxable Income	$81,500	$30,400
TAXES:		
Personal Tax	$18,917	$9,061
Corporate Tax	NIL	4,712
Total Tax	$18,917	$13,773
Net for lifestyle and investments	$61,083	$66,227

Prop Figure 7: Ontario proprietorship comparison table

The sole proprietor reports his net business income in his annual personal tax return and is taxed using the graduated tax brackets. The incorporated contractor can set his salary remuneration at any level required to meet his current lifestyle requirements. It is interesting to note that because the business is now paying for a lot of expenses that would be paid from after-tax income as an employee; a contractor does not require as high a salary as he had as an employee.

The Ontario incorporated contractor pays himself a salary of $51,100 and after taxes of $9,061 still has a net of $42,039 from this source. In addition, the company still retains $24,188 that can be invested within the company.

In the above table we have used a salary for the incorporated contractor's remuneration rather than a dividend or a salary/dividend combination. Doing so would improve the incorporated contractor's position relative to the proprietor in most provinces. Even using a salary for the remuneration, there is still a distinct financial advantage for the incorporated contractor. As the gross and net revenues increase, the discrepancy will grow as more and more of the proprietor's income will be taxed at higher marginal personal tax rates.

In the simple example set out above, the net savings in taxes through a corporation operating in Ontario is **$5,144 per year.**

Future Value of $5,144 per annum invested at a rate of 2.75%:

5 years	$ 27,174
10 years	$ 58,296
15 years	$ 93,939
25 years	$181,510

While artificial numbers have been used in the scenarios used here, my "average" incorporated independent contractor client in 2011 was grossing in excess of $130,000 and spending approximately $19,000 on expenses. The "average" figures are achieved by eliminating the top and bottom 20% of clients and using only the mid-sixty range.

Proprietorship/Corporation Comparisons – Newfoundland Tax Rates

We will look at a comparison of earning gross contract revenue of $100,000 in Newfoundland through a proprietorship and through a corporation. The assumptions and figures are similar to what we looked at in Chapter 2.

To make the comparison as simple as possible we will make some assumptions as follows:

1. The gross revenue is $100,000 for both the proprietor and for the corporation. There is no rate differential if you operate either way unless you are contracting through a placement firm. Operating expenses total $20,000 of which $3,000 is for meals and entertainment. Such expenses are tax deductible at only 50% of the actual expenditure.

2. The tax rates in effect are those for Newfoundland in 2012. As with the previous examples, we want to use flat rates for simplicity.

3. A salary is taken from the corporation set at $50,100 being the maximum level for 2012 CPP contributions. Please note that the CPP has been removed in the tax calculations below. As the salary for the incorporated contractor is set at the maximum for contributions, there should be no difference in

the net tax between the two options.

4. No Registered Retirement Savings Plan contributions (RRSPs) are considered.

	Proprietorship	Corporation
Gross Revenue	$100,000	$100,000
Less:		
Expenses	20,000	20,000
Salary	NIL	51,100
Net Income	$80,000	$28,900
Taxable Income	$81,500	$30,400
TAXES:		
Personal Tax	$20,551	$9,951
Corporate Tax	NIL	4,560
Total Tax	$20,551	$14,511
Net for lifestyle and investments	$59,449	$65,489

Prop Figure 8: Newfoundland Proprietorship comparison table

The sole proprietor reports his net business income in his annual personal tax return and is taxed using the graduated tax brackets. The incorporated contractor can set his salary remuneration at any level required to meet his current lifestyle requirements. It is interesting to note that because the business is now paying for a lot of expenses that would be paid from after-tax income as an employee; a contractor does not require as high a salary as he had as an employee.

The Newfoundland incorporated contractor pays himself a salary of $51,100 and after taxes of $9,951 still has a net of $41,149 from this source. In addition, the company still retains $24,340 that can be invested within the company.

In the above table we have used a salary for the incorporated contractor's remuneration rather than a dividend or a salary/dividend combination. Doing so would improve the incorporated contractor's position relative to the proprietor in most provinces. Even using a salary for the remuneration, there is still a distinct financial advantage for the incorporated contractor. As the gross and net revenues increase, the discrepancy will grow as more and more of the proprietor's income will be taxed at higher marginal personal tax rates.

In the simple example set out above, the net savings in taxes through a corporation operating in Newfoundland is **$6,040 per year.**

Future Value of $6,040 per annum invested at a rate of 2.75%:

5 years	$ 31,907
10 years	$ 68,450
15 years	$110,301
25 years	$213,127

While artificial numbers have been used in the scenarios used here, my "average" incorporated independent contractor client in 2011 was grossing in excess of $130,000 and spending approximately $19,000 on expenses. The "average" figures are achieved by eliminating the top and bottom 20% of clients and using only the mid-sixty range.

Dennis R. Dowling

Dennis R. Dowling is a Chartered Professional Accountant (Chartered Accountant – Alberta) and Certified Financial Planner.

Dennis graduated with honours Bachelor of Commerce degree from Queen's University at Kingston in 1971. He articled with a national accounting firm in Kingston before transferring with the firm to Edmonton in 1978. After short management stints in the banking industry and with the Alberta Institute of Chartered Accountants, he joined a local accounting firm and became a partner in 1983.

Dennis worked extensively with independent contractors in his accounting practice between 1996 and his retirement in late 2011. As at his retirement, Dennis had a clientele that included approximately 350 corporate independent contractors. He accumulated over 14,000 hours of face to face meetings with independent contractors and has written numerous articles on independent contracting for his clients and one of the major information technology organizations. He has presented various seminars for prospective contractors and specifically for his clients.

Dennis was a co-founding partner of a national Chartered Accounting firm in 2003. He was the managing partner of the Edmonton office and chaired the national firm's independent contractor committee until his retirement.

CPSIA information can be obtained at www.ICGtesting.com
Printed in the USA
LVOW11s0714291014

410925LV00003B/16/P

9 781460 210758